THE MONSTROUS TRICK

The Monstrous Trick

Kenneth McDonald

APEC Books Ltd.

First published in 1998 by
APEC Books Ltd.
3080 Yonge Street, Suite 5040
Toronto, Ontario
Canada, M4N 3N1

Cover design by
Rebecca Marsh-Pelzl

Printed in Canada by
Webcom
3480 Pharmacy Avenue
Scarborough, Ontario
Canada, M1W 3G3

The publisher received no financial assistance for this project.

Canadian Cataloguing In Publication Data

McDonald, Kenneth, 1914-
    The monstrous trick

Includes bibliographical references and index.
ISBN 0-9695634-2-6

1. Federal-provincial relations – Quebec (Province).* 2. Canada – English-French relations. 3. Federal government – Canada. 4. Canada - Constitutional history. 5. Canada – Politics and government – 1984-1993.* 6. Canada – Politics and government – 1993- .* I. Title.

FC144.M28 1998   320.471'049   C98-933036-2
F1027.M28 1998

The most important change which extensive government control produces is a psychological change, an alteration in the character of the people. This is necessarily a slow affair, a process which extends not over a few years but perhaps over one or two generations.

- Friedrich Hayek

· FOREWORD ·

Canadians' politeness and generosity incline them to swallow the myths of Quebecers' sufferings at the hands of les maudits anglais and to accept the costs of appeasement.

Nevertheless to continue the appeasement is to fly in the face of history. From the Danegeld to Munich, appeasement's record is unchanged: compromise in the face of superior force leads only to surrender.

It has led Canadians to acquiesce in the monstrous trick played upon them by a handful of political schemers from the regional minority of French Canadians anchored in Quebec.

By a combination of stealth and political acumen they overthrew Canada's system of government and replaced it by Quebec's statist model of legislated rights and entitlements under a central authority.

In the thirty years from 1967 to 1997 Canadians' centuries-old tradition of inherent freedom and responsibility under the common law and sovereign parliaments was effectively undermined.

Since the Quebec model includes what Quebec Premier Lucien Bouchard has called Quebecers' "marked tendency to favour a more peaceful option than the rest of Canada in defence matters," this radical change has been accompanied by such a shrinkage of the armed forces that, if the army were called upon to give aid to the civil power in two parts of Canada, it would have to choose between them because it couldn't handle both at once.

Couple this with Quebec's move toward sovereignty, as well as a strengthening and militancy of labour unions masquerading as "social movements" in open defiance of elected governments, and the threat to civil order is transparent.

The book calls upon the Canadian majority to stiffen its collective spine and generate political leaders with a similar resolve.

Kenneth McDonald

•CONTENTS•

Chapter 1

How it was done

Canada's enemies of the past were driven by combinations of state power in the hands of proud men in Europe.

Only 36 years after V-E Day, proud men of its own used state power to overturn Canada's system of government.

Without either their prior consent or subsequent approval, Canadians were duped into ceding rule to a minority.

This was the monstrous trick.

Radicals from the French Canadian minority that is anchored in Quebec contrived to substitute their civil code model of legislated rights and entitlements for Canada's common law tradition of inherent freedom and responsibility under a sovereign Parliament.

In Canada's federal system, political power was divided between the federal government in Ottawa and governments in the provincial capitals.

Ottawa's responsibilities were national in scope.

Provincial governments were responsible for property and civil rights and "generally all matters of a merely local or private nature in the province."

In short, the division of powers delivered what author Felix Morley called "the essence of federalism" by reserving control over local affairs to the localities themselves.

In Canada's circumstances this enabled Quebec to practice within the province its civil code tradition of centralized authority and the use of French.

In the 1960s, radicals from Quebec set out to change the federal system of divided powers into one that matched their contrary tradition of a centralized authority.

After they had infiltrated the federal government they would extend its power over the whole country by entrenching a charter of collective rights and freedoms - especially language rights - as Canada's supreme law.

To do this, the radicals planted their socialist roots in the national Liberal Party, and propelled one of their own - Pierre Elliott Trudeau - to succeed Lester Pearson in the seat of power: the office of Prime Minister.

In Canada, the power of a prime minister who controls a

majority in the House of Commons is as all-encompassing as he chooses to make it.

Through his power as party leader to sign or refrain from signing MPs' nomination papers before an election, he dominates the party's parliamentary caucus. He alone decides when an election is to be called. He puts the final stamp both upon party policy and upon party tactics in the Commons.

In an age that has bred professional politicians, those of the governing party know that their chances of promotion and in fact their whole careers depend solely upon the prime minister's opinion of their usefulness to him.

Former prime minister Lester Pearson's oft-quoted remark that a Canadian prime minister with an assured majority is the nearest thing to a dictator - "if he wants to be one" - was a true statement, yet even without an assured majority Pearson made radical changes of his own.

By forcing through a British-style national health scheme, and following it with other "universal" social programs, he subverted Canada's federal system of government and set the course for insolvency.

By legitimizing the myth of "two founding races" (English and French) he set the course for secession.

Until then, the prevailing view was that, over time, the forces of faction and party dissolved into a middle way that (like the common law which is the fruit of parliaments) kept pace with the times and avoided extremes.

That was the Canadian way until Quebec's Quiet Revolution of the 1960s and the accompanying rise of French Canadian nationalism moved Pearson into the path of appeasement. He established a Royal Commission on Bilingualism and Biculturalism and recruited Quebec's "Three Wise Men", (Jean Marchand, Gérard Pelletier, and Pierre Trudeau) to his cause.

That they were also Men of the Left, bent on changing the country at its foundations, was an extension of Pearson's own changes; his chosen successor completed the job in little more than a decade.

The committed socialist whose close friend Gérard Pelletier said that he had devoted his whole thinking since the age of 14 toward politics and the use of power ("He knows where he is going and why")[1] set about using the power of his office right from the start. His first step toward sapping the supremacy of Parliament was to change the rules of procedure.

One of Pierre Trudeau's first acts as Prime Minister in 1968 was to introduce a package of parliamentary reform which included a restriction of question period that would have limited debate before it began.

When the Opposition in and outside Parliament protested - veteran MP Stanley Knowles called it a "desecration of the parliamentary process" - that proposal was withdrawn, but the rest of the package was passed. Trudeau said: "We pulled the ground out from under them, and Parliament has a completely new set of rules."[2]

The next year he reintroduced the rule that had been withdrawn, used his majority to impose closure on debate and passed the limiting rule - a forerunner of 1981 when he used his majority to force the Charter's preparatory resolution into the committee stage and thus to eventual passage.

Given the political instincts of the players, the outcome was predictable. Confronted with a rise of nationalism in Quebec, Lester Pearson's instinct was to appease the nationalists.

His Royal Commission on Bilingualism and Biculturalism was "to recommend what steps should be taken to develop the Canadian Confederation on the basis of an equal partnership between the two founding races."

That "the two founding races" were founded in myth owes much to a misreading of Lord Durham's celebrated description of "two nations warring in the bosom of a single state." He was referring not to Canada but to Quebec.[3]

Pearson's Royal Commission legitimized the myth.

What had been described by Robert Baldwin as "the voluntary choice of a free people" and later by Sir John A. Macdonald as "the Confederation of one people and one government instead of five peoples and five governments" was now split in two. The British North America Act's wise provision of a parliamentary democracy within a federal system had been undermined.

The essence of the BNA Act was the award of separate and exclusive powers to the two senior levels of government.

The federal government's powers affected the whole of Canada in such matters as criminal justice, defence, finance, foreign affairs, taxation, trade and commerce.

Provincial governments were responsible for such matters as borrowing on the sole credit of the province, law enforcement, direct taxation, education and health, municipal affairs, property and civil rights.[4]

The inherent freedom of all Canadians under the *federal* government was recognized in the BNA Act's provision that the provinces were "to be federally united into One Dominion...with a Constitution similar in principle to that of the United Kingdom."

The United Kingdom's unwritten constitution is rooted in the citizens' inherent freedom and responsibility under the common law. The common law, in turn, consists of precedents established both by parliamentary statutes and by the courts.

In short, the common law forms the framework of society. Parliamentary statutes and court decisions reflect the prevailing opinions of elected representatives and of the citizens who serve on juries. Consequently, the unwritten constitution keeps pace with the times.

That was the democratic umbrella under which the two-thirds of Canadians who inhabited the English-speaking provinces of Canada, and whose provincial governments followed the common law tradition, lived comfortably with the one-third of Canadians who inhabited Quebec and whose provincial governments followed the civil code tradition.

Assigning exclusive powers to provincial governments ensured that Quebecers' traditional dominance by a superior authority - first the Church and later the State - was recognized and provided for. Duly elected Quebec provincial governments had exclusive jurisdiction over property and civil rights and "generally all matters of a merely local or private nature."

In short, the matters which later became so prominent in *national* debate, namely language and culture, were constitutionally confined to the jurisdiction of the provinces. Religious differences were recognized by Section 93 of the BNA Act's protection of Separate Schools for "the Queen's Roman Catholic Subjects" in Upper Canada the same as for Dissentient Schools for "the Queen's Protestant and Roman Catholic Subjects in Quebec."

Section 133 provided that either the English or French language "may be used" in the Canadian Parliament, the Quebec Legislature, in any federal court and the courts of Quebec, and that both languages "shall be used" in the Canadian and Quebec legislatures' respective journals.

Thus do we see how the "two founding races" myth and its later extension into two official languages for the whole country conflicted with the federal system of divided powers.

The federal system automatically protected the language, culture, and authoritarian form of government that was peculiar to French Canadians in Quebec.

Surrounded on the North American continent by an audio-visual print and electronic world of English, French Canadians' opportunities to learn English were boundless; whereas in the provinces and territories of English Canada, French was rarely heard or spoken.

Pierre Trudeau's excuse for imposing English-French bilingualism through a Charter was to combat French Canadian nationalism. Making the country "irreversibly bilingual" would open up the whole of Canada to French Canadians.

In the event, his language legislation, and its later entrenchment in a Charter, did three things. First, it catered to what Richard Gwyn called "the distinctive breed" of upper middle-class francophones and their anglophone counterparts, mostly from Montreal, who had learned the other language in childhood. Second, it encouraged other French Canadians who lived within reach of English media to exploit their natural advantage by becoming bilingual; and, third, it qualified them automatically to fill the newly created "bilingual" positions in the civil and armed services.

Soon, official bilingualism began to appeal to elites in English Canada as well. The effect was to create a "New Class" of politicians, bureaucrats, academics and journalists who bought into bilingualism as the means to personal advancement.

They, who so strongly influence the tone of public debate, have everything to gain from focussing that debate on "the Quebec problem." Their interest must always be to "keep Quebec in Canada," so that they can continue their crusade of appeasing their mirror images in Quebec - its nationalists - whose demands for concessions are equally persistent.

Both participants in this phoney war are driven by similar emotions: personal ambition, lust for power, conviction that they know what is best for the people at large (whether in Canada as a whole, or within the confines of Quebec) and a determination to keep the phoney war going.

Implicit on both sides is a need to prevent the masses from learning one another's history, language, or tradition; propagating the New Class's versions is essential to effective control. Thus the 65 percent of Quebec's people who are unilingual in French can be bombarded with a nationalist version of history. At the same time,

English Canada's people can be swamped with tales of Quebec's sufferings; and swamped also by waves of immigrants who are encouraged to import and perpetuate the customs of the countries they came from.

These two elements of Canada's New Class are mirror images of one another, both dedicated to keeping the war going for the sake of their careers.

In 1969, the Official Languages Act spread "official bilingualism" over the whole country. Henceforward, fluency in French was to be the criterion for advancement not only in the civil and armed services but also "in all the institutions of the Parliament and Government of Canada."

Since Trudeau was already embarked on creating new ministries and "a furtive expansion of central agencies," this ensured their eventual domination by French Canadians.

It also intruded on the provincial preserves of English and French Canadians alike, and undermined the federal system.

That it failed to appease the nationalists, while antagonizing the Canadian majority, all at huge cost to the community, is a matter of record.

As a parliamentary statute the Official Languages Act might have been amended or repealed by a later Parliament.

It was the threat of repeal that drove Pierre Trudeau to engineer his revolutionary change.

In 1981-2, without having sought a mandate from Canadians in the preceding general election, he incorporated the language laws in a Charter of Rights and Freedoms that constitutional authority Senator Eugene Forsey said was so rigid as to be almost impossible to amend.[5]

The Charter was the centrepiece of the "patriation" deception of 1981-2.

Canada had been a self-governing Dominion since passage of the Statute of Westminster in 1931. The only reason why Canada still sent its constitutional amendments to Westminster - where they were automatically approved - was successive Canadian governments' failure to reach agreement with the provinces on a formula for amending the Constitution in Canada.

This *Canadian* failure was twisted by Pierre Trudeau and his fellow strategists into a *colonial* relic which could only be resolved by "patriating" the BNA Act to Canada by means of a Canada Bill passed by the British Parliament.

But entrenched in the Canada Bill was the Charter of Rights and Freedoms which incorporated Trudeau's treasured language rights: his Official Languages Act of 1969 would be forever preserved from parliamentary repeal.

In debates on the Canada Bill, Britain's foremost constitutional authority, the Rt. Hon. J. Enoch Powell, made two significant comments.

He said that as "an entrenched and justiciable document, a charter of liberties or a bill of rights is incompatible with parliamentary sovereignty."

He called the Trudeau stratagem "a tool to produce political results in Canada that could not have been produced without that form of deception."[6]

Designated as the Supreme Law of Canada, the Charter also incorporated an amending formula together with the redistributive mechanisms and state-ordained equalizations of socialism which characterized the statist tradition of Quebec.

By a cleverly planned deception of the Canadian public, the statist tradition of the regional minority anchored in Quebec had been imposed on the whole of Canada - and Quebec's government refused to sign it because it invaded the province's exclusive powers. (It was signed by the Queen of Canada and three federal MPs from Quebec: Pierre Trudeau, Jean Chrétien, and André Ouellet.)

Since then, an exodus from Quebec of Canadians favouring the British tradition and an influx of immigrants to English Canada have reduced Quebec's original third of the population to barely a quarter, of which a little more than half, perhaps 13 percent of the Canadian total, are said to favour secession from Canada in a separate state.

The percentage of French Canadians who want to secede represents more than half the French Canadian population of Quebec, but its voting power is watered down by non-secessionist French Canadians, anglophones and allophones who live in the province.

What no one knows is the answer to these questions:
1. How many of the dissidents who reply to pollsters and vote in referendums believe that a separate Quebec will keep all of the present provincial territory?
2. How many of them believe that things will be much the same after separation - Canadian dollar,

Canadian passports, free trade with Canada and the
USA, access to Canadian health services, and so on?
3. How many of them believe that by voting for
   sovereignty they are merely strengthening their own
   provincial government's hand in squeezing more
   concessions from Ottawa?

Throughout the thirty-year period, Quebecers' political acumen,
which they express by voting strategically in federal elections, gave
them not only a disproportionate share of the spoils but also, for all
but one of the 30 years after Pearson's retirement, a prime minister
from Quebec.

The regional minority's numbers might be declining, but the
decline was more than offset by the rise of its power over the
Canadian majority; power exercised throughout by Quebec-based
prime ministers and their obedient governments.

Canada's mix of a parliamentary democracy within a federal
system enabled Quebecers to exert political influence in Ottawa to
their material advantage at the cost of a corresponding political
intrusion upon the exclusive powers that the federal system secured to
their native province.

This is the paradox that bedevils the Canadian state: the
province whose majority francophone population regards it as the
home of the French Canadian race in Canada regards itself also as an
equal partner in the affairs of the country in which the francophones
of Quebec are a regional minority.

Yet Quebec's political influence in Ottawa, coupled with the
near-dictatorial power of prime ministers from Quebec, culminated in
1981-2, to use Pierre Trudeau's words, in "almost a putsch, a coup de
force"[7] that changed Canada's system of government to the Quebec
model.

So signal a defeat at the hands of a determined minority has
demoralized the English Canadian majority to such a degree that this
once-great country is now said to be distinguished not by its having
created civilization out of the wilderness, nor by its unequalled record
in two world wars, but by the social programs which bundled it into a
per capita national debt almost three times that of the US.[8]

Parliamentary democracy comprises two important features. The
first is that the majority rules. The British tradition of inherent
freedom and responsibility under the common law ensures that
minorities are treated justly; the majority does not oppress them. But

when affairs of state reach the floor of Parliament for a decision, it is the voice of the majority that decides. The second feature is that, although the people elect representatives to speak for them, the power remains with the people. They elect representatives to debate, and eventually decide, the issues, but those they elect are still representatives, never their masters.

Within that tradition, the regional minority in Quebec was treated justly. Education rights of "the Queen's Roman Catholic subjects" were preserved and either English or French could be used in Parliament, in the Quebec Legislature and in federal and Quebec courts.

Quebecers were free to practice their form of government within the province. The BNA Act's division of powers secured to them, as it did to all provinces, exclusive powers over matters, notably property and civil rights, that were peculiar to the province.

However, Pearson's legitimizing of the two founding races myth could hardly fail to intensify the spirit of nationalism in Quebec. Moved by what Henri Bourassa had called "a national tradition of three centuries," the nationalists began to agitate for independence.

This brought them head to head with Pierre Trudeau, who was strongly opposed to nationalism of any kind because it stood in the way of the international redistributions that would evolve from the socialism to which he was committed in Canada.

His antidote for Quebec nationalism was to make the whole country "irreversibly bilingual."

Pockets of francophones across the land would be subsidized to spread the use of French, their numbers would be augmented by French Canadians exported from Quebec to fill positions in Trudeau's "furtive expansion of federal agencies," and civil and armed service positions would be categorized as "bilingual" to attract francophones from Quebec.

The regional minority would permeate and effectively rule the majority in a Canada that would fit into the forthcoming federation of the world.

However, this did nothing to appease the nationalists; they saw their heritage, and their future, in the soil of Quebec. They still do.

Nevertheless, Trudeau pressed on with his vision of an irreversibly bilingual country. In his commitment to socialism he was a true Quebecer. Socialism's centralization of authority which also characterizes the French tradition comes naturally to Quebecers emerging from the guardianship of the Church to that of the State.

9

That socialism is incompatible with a federal state of divided powers applies only to the federal government; provincial governments can practice it at will.

The proof lies in Quebec itself, where successive governments pride themselves on their "social democratic" persuasion, as have governments in other provinces from time to time, notably Saskatchewan and British Columbia.

The underpinnings of leftist governments are rooted in sympathy with labour unions that give them financial support, and an inclination toward state-financed and state-regulated boards and commissions with wide powers over industry, trade and commerce, all with the object of redistributing whatever wealth is created so as to "equalize" material benefits.

That this is a viable proposition within the territory of a province has been demonstrated frequently by Saskatchewan, whose social democratic governments have disciplined themselves to observe and practice fiscal rectitude.

The regime may not produce as much wealth as a classical liberal approach that favours individual effort over that of the collective, but provided the *federal* government practices fiscal rectitude through its monetary and budgetary policies, the provincial economy will jog along at its chosen pace.

This brings us back to the Canadian paradox. It was when Quebec's influence on national policy bent the Pearson government the same way, and when one of the "Three Wise Men" from Quebec who had advised Pearson succeeded him as prime minister, that the *federal* government was committed to the practices of redistribution and equalization that are incompatible with a federal state.

Thus when Quebec's nationalists seek "freedom" from the oppressive Canadian state, the oppression they resent is self-inflicted. It has nothing to do with the federal ideal of divided powers; it has everything to do with Quebec's own dominance over Canadian governments and those governments' consequent centralization of political authority in the Quebec mode that conflicts with the federal ideal.

The freedom of provincial governments to use their exclusive powers over property and civil rights, which included language and culture, was also bound to conflict with the plan to spread the use of French.

Despite entry into the statutes of the Official Languages Act that declared English and French to be the official languages of Canada, that statute, like any other, could be amended or repealed by a later parliament.

Therefore, in his fourth term of office, and without having sought a mandate during the election campaign for such a radical change, Trudeau put his language law beyond the reach of Parliament by incorporating it in a Charter of Rights and Freedoms in the French mode of legislated rights and entitlements as the Supreme Law of Canada.

Thus has the English Canadian majority been brought to a condition wherein its treasured thousand-year heritage of inherent freedom and responsibility under laws that moved with the times has been changed 180 degrees without its consent or subsequent approval. And it was done by political schemers from the regional minority to cement that minority's power over the whole country.

The astonishing thing about that manoeuvre is not so much that it succeeded as that the Canadian majority appears to have acquiesced. Criticism of the method, opposition to the imposed system itself - these are confined to a handful of articles by percipient lawyers and a book or two by conservative authors.

Yet the gulf between the French system of centralized authority and the British tradition of inherent freedom and responsibility under the evolving common law was the subject of spirited debate in France and England before and during the French Revolution.

Then, the French could have followed the English example of 1689 - The Glorious Revolution - that made the King's title dependent upon an Act of Parliament.

After Louis XVI recalled the Estates-General in 1789 the delegates could have proceeded, as the years passed, to bring the laws, especially those affecting civil rights, the authority of the Crown and of the ancient institution of the Estates-General itself, into keeping with the spirit of the times; in short, into a constitutional monarchy after the English model.

Instead the radicals embarked on fundamental change that culminated in the Reign of Terror, the cause, author R.J. Rummel estimates, of 263,000 deaths between 1793-94.[9]

Moreover, the French author René Sédillot has argued in a 1987 book about the cost of the Revolution, that the Terror "may have presaged the great holocausts of recent times" and that "it turned France into a centralized state; an administrative malady from which it still suffers."[10]

Canada has been injected with the same malady. Its new

Constitution embodies the conflicting imperatives of freedom and state-mandated equality, sets out the confines of a paternalistic welfare state in which enforcing the spread of the French language takes precedence over individual rights and freedoms, and incorporates an "amending formula" that makes the whole document almost impossible to amend.

During the Quebec referendum campaign on sovereignty of 1995, elected provincial and federal representatives in English Canada were warned not to interfere, and the few who spoke out on the topic were censured by the establishment press as well as by "federalist" politicians from Quebec.

A favourite theme of the latter was to remind Quebecers of the leading role played by their provincial representatives in Canadian institutions.

For example, in the preceding 27 years, the prime minister of Canada had been a Quebecer for 25 of them. At the time of the referendum, Quebecers held the posts of Ambassador to the United States; Chief of Staff to the Prime Minister; Clerk of the Privy Council; Chief of the Defence Staff; Commissioner of Official Languages; Auditor-General; Director of the Canada Council; President of the Canadian International Development Agency; and Chief Justice of the Supreme Court.

There were five cabinet ministers from Quebec, including the senior post of Finance Minister, as well as another 15 Quebecers in the Liberal caucus, many Quebecers headed civil service departments as deputy ministers and assistant deputy ministers, the whole of the Official Opposition was from Quebec, and the Governor-General was a francophone.

All this was offered to Quebecers as proof that the existing system worked for them, while the representatives of the Canadian majority that constitutes English Canada were enjoined to keep quiet.

In fact, that paragraph sums up Canada's problem. Under the guise of being "fair" to Quebec, and making amends for "200 years of injustice," the Canadian majority has not merely allowed itself to be bent over backwards but to be so twisted out of shape as to be unrecognizable.

French Canada runs the government. The French language is mandated for use by government and its agencies throughout the country's capital to the extent that Dr. Marguerite Ritchie, President of the Human Rights Institute of Canada, admitted during a panel discussion in 1995 that there is no longer a career for anglophones in the federal civil service in Canada. By the following year francophone civil servants in the national capital region had reached 38 percent of the total. By contrast, anglophone residents in Quebec comprised less than one percent of the provincial government service.

Thus do we see the result of strategy implemented by an admirer of Mao Tse-tung (Pierre Trudeau called him "that superb strategist")[11]

- **first**, by changing the rules for advancement in the federal government service from "by merit" to "by language and heritage" (bilingual meant francophone);
- **second**, by establishing government-subsidized francophone enclaves throughout English-speaking Canada to serve as conduits for the redistributive politics that socialism requires;
- **third**, by centralizing authority in Ottawa by "the most furtive expansion of central agencies the world has yet experienced"[12];
- and finally, by imposing on Canadians a Constitution in the French mode of government-guaranteed, but limited, "rights and freedoms" that substitutes rights and entitlements for responsibilities.

All of the foregoing is in the French tradition of centralized authority which is fundamentally incompatible with a federal state and with parliamentary sovereignty.

In 1995 we saw the inevitable outcome of the Charter's declaration (52.1) that any law inconsistent with its provisions "is, to the extent of the inconsistency, of no force or effect." At para. 92 of *Hill vs. Church of Scientology of Toronto, July 20, 1995*, the Supreme Court of Canada wrote:

Historically, the common law evolved as a result of the courts making those incremental changes which were necessary in order to make the law comply with current societal values. The Charter represents a restatement of the fundamental values which guide and shape our democratic society and our legal system. It follows that it is appropriate for the courts to make such incremental revisions to the common law as may be necessary to have it comply with the values enunciated in the Charter.

No longer will the law move with the times; instead not only new law (which, as we shall see, the unelected judges propose to make), but the immemorial common law itself are all to be squeezed into the changeless mold of the unamendable Charter.

The evolving common law was rooted in negative rights. Certain acts were prohibited and carried penalties in line with their judicial heritage in the commandments God delivered to Moses and which were later interpreted by Jesus. But since 1982, when the Charter was imposed on Canadians, laws which are obscure and ambiguous declare positive rights and entitlements that people can claim through the courts.

The difference is plain: negative rights leave decisions about abiding by or breaking the law to the individual; positive rights put decisions in the hands of the state, its tribunals and commissions, and its unelected judges.

On April 20, 1982, on the second floor of the West Block in the Parliament Buildings, broadcaster Joel Aldred made a note of the words he had just exchanged with former Supreme Court chief justice the Right Honourable Bora Laskin.

Mr. Laskin recalled his prediction of the previous year when Mr. Trudeau was pressing for his Charter of Rights and Freedoms to be incorporated in a written constitution. At that time, Mr. Laskin said: "After the Canadian Bill of Rights we had twenty years of good jurisprudence. I predict that after the proposed Charter of Rights and Freedoms we will have fifty years of dissent."[13]

Mr. Laskin's prediction is fulfilled in the proliferation of groups, often funded by the state, whose "protests" against this or that perceived offence by individuals or institutions are the stuff of headlines in the nation's print and electronic media.

It is fulfilled in illegal strikes called by labour union leaders desperate to keep the power they wield over members who are forced by law to pay dues to the unions.

It is fulfilled in Liberal governments' abrogation of lawful contracts and their habitual breach, following electoral victories, of promises made to the electorate.

The encroachment of Canada's federal government upon the provinces' constitutional power over property and civil rights began with Lester Pearson's imposition of "universal" medicare, soon to be followed by an array of "social programs" in the socialist mode of redistributing wealth and incomes.

This radical change from inherent freedom and responsibility to state dependency was accompanied inevitably by a gradual growth of the size and influence of government's presence.

The emphasis upon rights and entitlements shifted Canadians away from the habit of settling their differences face to face; instead they began to litigate, and looked to the state to fund their actions.

Gradually the concept of state dependency drew them to think of themselves less as individuals and more as members of groups that were later identified in the Charter: groups that were "socially or economically disadvantaged," or groups that were "disadvantaged because of race, national or ethnic origin, colour, religion, sex, age or mental or physical disability."

Aggravating the shift was uncertainty about the law itself. The ambiguities of the Charter were noted by Enoch Powell: "Certainly, no one reading the generalities of [the Charter] could possibly decide how a court would rule upon so many measures which in legislation we are careful by procedure to define as accurately and precisely, and often intelligently, as we can."[14]

If people cannot be sure what the law requires, if, as they would be justified in suspecting, the law is so complicated and so vague in its possible applications that they will never understand it, they will go to great lengths to avoid contention by stating their opinions about anything. Nor is it only the formal law that intimidates them. Why risk censure for the sake of speaking or writing your mind about a public issue when you know that this or that interest group is watching or listening to every media outlet, ready on the instant to detect and condemn the slightest hint of criticism in terms that liken you to a redneck, a fascist or a bigot - and when the print and electronic press is just as ready to report it?

Reinforcing the intimidation is another ruling by the Supreme Court of Canada in *Hill v. Church of Scientology of Toronto*, July 20, 1995. At para 137 the Court wrote:

I simply cannot see that the law of defamation is unduly restrictive or inhibiting. Surely it is not requiring too much of individuals that they ascertain the truth of the allegations they publish.

For an individual, at his or her own expense, to be obliged to "ascertain the truth" of something spoken or written against attack by one or another of the state-funded groups that have nothing better to do than winkle out deemed slurs on their private interest - is nothing but a thinly disguised attack on free speech.

It is also an attack on what I had always thought to be an

outstanding feature of the Canadian character; namely, to speak one's mind without fear or favour.

My first exposure to Canadians was in England in the late 1930s when the Royal Air Force was expanding. Sprinkled among the candidates for short service commissions as pilots were Canadians who had worked their passages across the Atlantic (and many of them across Canada first) on the chance of being accepted.

They were quiet, polite but businesslike, and two particularly - Homer Cochrane and Johnny McKid - were outstanding rugby players. Later, when I had seen those personal qualities reinforced at Camp Borden and other places, I came to recognize them as national characteristics.

Polite, but blunt when necessary, practical and down to earth, independent but ready to help (but not to interfere), not class conscious: these were the features that distinguished Canadians from other people and were the foundation of an effort in the Second World War that for sheer productivity was unmatched by any Allied nation.

Polite, but blunt when necessary. How does that square with our latter-day learned judges' preachments about ascertaining the truth of everything before we open our mouths? How does it square with freely expressed *opinions*?

When Johnny McKid learned that I'd been posted to Canada as an instructor he said, "Mac, you're going to civilization." Johnny was a graduate aeronautical engineer from the universities of Alberta and Washington, and he was killed on April 27, 1942, during his second tour of operations, after winning the DFC on his first, when 31 Halifaxes and 12 Lancasters attacked the *Tirpitz* and other German warships in Trondheim Fjord.

Homer Cochrane won a bar to his DFC commanding a fighter squadron in the Western Desert; he survived the war only to be killed in a flying accident in the 1950s.

Bill Carr, the fine air force officer we shall meet again, told me that when he was leading the service team in discussions about the Canadian-led multinational project that eventually produced the Tornado, the Germans particularly welcomed Canada's leadership because, Bill said, "They knew we could be blunt and demanding with the British" who had other ideas about the design.

I watched Bill Carr at first hand in Denmark, where I had been selling Canadair's capability as a manufacturing source for the project, and he came to brief the Danes on it: clear, straight to the point, no nonsense.

That was 30 years ago and just the other day a friend who had been a rear gunner in Halifaxes lamented to me that he and his fellow Canadians "have lost the habit of speaking out."

Canada's so-called public arena has become a breeding ground for state-mandated commissions and committees and tribunals whose purpose in life is to hear the complaints of state-funded or subsidized groups of people who feel themselves disadvantaged or discriminated against by other people or institutions, or whose condition has been insufficiently ameliorated by one or another of the state's laws, programs or activities.

The source of, and justification for their complaints is Equality Rights in section 15 of the Charter, rights, incidentally, which can be abrogated by Parliament or a provincial legislature through use of the "notwithstanding clause" of the same Charter.

Now the inspiration for the Charter is in the French civil code and the top-down, centralized form of government ingrained in the Quebec politicians who planted the thing on us. It is therefore entirely logical that the federal language law (Bill C-72) which replaced the Official Languages Act in 1988 should copy the arbitrary provisions of Quebec's Bill 101 which made French the official language of Quebec.

Under Quebec's Bill 101 adherence was enforced - offenders being liable to fines that increased for subsequent offences - by a French language office and a surveillance commission known locally as the language police.

Under Ottawa's Bill C-72 "the Commissioner...may apply to the Court for a remedy in relation to a complaint" and the government can prescribe "anything that [it] considers necessary to effect compliance with this Act."

Under Quebec's Bill 101 none of the enforcement staff's members could be prosecuted for acts connected with their official duties.

Under Ottawa's Bill C-72 the Commissioner is protected against any action for libel or slander.

Under Quebec's Bill 101 the identity of any complainant reporting a breach of the law would be protected.

Under Ottawa's Bill C-72 the Commissioner could not be called as a witness.

Although the whole tale reeks of arbitrary powers, it is those last four sentences that frighten me. That the Government of Canada has copied the Government of Quebec by encouraging Canadians to spy on one another secure in the knowledge that they will not be identified or called as a witness is contrary to everything we know and feel about justice.

But it is entirely in keeping with the French penal code that protects public servants from prosecution for anything done in discharge of their official duties.[15] It is also in keeping with the basis on which totalitarian states depend to keep their people in subjection.

It is not a difference in kind but merely one of degree that distinguishes the powers of Canada's and Quebec's language police from those of their forerunners not only in the Europe of the 1930s and 1940s but also in the Soviet Union where, from 1917 until its collapse in the 1980s, innocent people were arrested; "naturally - otherwise no one would be frightened."[16]

Canada's language laws are but one example of the incremental growth of the State. How their effect upon individual freedom is reinforced by other laws, by the Charter itself, and by interpretations in the courts, tribunals and commissions of an increasingly litigious country will be examined in the next chapter.

Chapter 2

How the Charter entrenches growth of the state

Russell Juriansz, who worked for ten years as an in-house lawyer for Canada's federal Human Rights Commission, said that human rights commissions have no incentive to throw out groundless complaints; their interest is "to maximize the number of complaints that they deal with statistically. Then they can say they get lots of complaints, and thus need more funding."[1]

On November 28, 1995, *The Globe and Mail* reported that University of Western Ontario Psychology Professor J. Philippe Rushton's ordeal at the hands of his state-sponsored persecutors had ended.

Since January 1989, when he presented an oral paper at the annual meeting of the American Association for the Advancement of Science in San Francisco, Rushton had been hounded by a variety of "Equality" and "Race Relations" groups to recant from the findings of his research, and the university administration forced him to teach classes by videotape, allegedly for his own protection.

Rushton's "crime" was his publication of scientific evidence that Orientals are intellectually superior to Caucasians, who in turn are superior to Blacks.

That cognitive ability is a general factor on which humans differ, that it is measurable and substantially heritable, was examined later and at great length by Richard J. Herrnstein and Charles Murray in their 1994 book *The Bell Curve*. In a brief comment on Rushton's work they wrote that "As science, there is nothing wrong with Rushton's work in principle; we expect that time will tell whether it is right or wrong in fact."[2]

After all the assaults on Rushton had foundered on Ontario Attorney General Ian Scott's announcement, following a six-month investigation, that no charges would be laid under either the hate law or the false news law, several students laid a complaint against the university with the Ontario Human Rights Commission on grounds of Rushton's alleged "racism."

Four years later, on November 28, 1995, the *Globe* reported that the complaint had "petered out." The Commission was unable to locate any of the 19 people who had lodged the complaint. Their lawyer said they had "fled to all corners of the world" since 1991.

With remarkable restraint, Professor Rushton said he was obviously pleased "but it does leave a slight negative aftertaste that there has been such an inquiry in the first place."

In the late 1960s, Canada's Criminal Code was amended by the addition of two new sections 318 and 319 under the heading Hate Propaganda. Section 319 deals with Public Incitement of Hatred and it states:

    (1) Every one who, by communicating statements in any public place, incites hatred against any identifiable group where such incitement is likely to lead to a breach of the peace is guilty of

      (a) an indictable offence and is liable to imprisonment for a term not exceeding two years; or

      (b) an offence punishable on summary conviction.

    (2) Every one who, by communicating statements, other than in private conversation, wilfully promotes hatred against any identifiable group is guilty of

      (a) an indictable offence and is liable to imprisonment for a term not exceeding two years; or

      (b) an offence punishable on summary conviction.

    (3) No person shall be convicted of an offence under subsection (2)

      (a) if he establishes that the statements communicated were true;

      (b) if, in good faith, he expressed or attempted to establish by argument an opinion on a religious subject;

      (c) if the statements were relevant to any subject of public interest, the discussion of which was for the public benefit, and if on reasonable grounds he believed them to be true; or

      (d) if, in good faith, he intended to point out, for the purpose of removal, matters producing or tending to produce feelings of hatred toward an identifiable group in Canada.

My reaction to those three paragraphs is that they wouldn't be needed if everyone adhered to what I've suggested before are Canadians' inherent characteristics, foremost of which is being polite to other people but blunt when necessary.

What civilized person would stand in a public place or before a microphone and incite hatred against an identifiable group? What, apart from the implicit presumption that the group he belonged to was superior to the other one, would be the point? And even if he were sufficiently foolish or prejudiced or falsely proud as to do such a thing, who would pay any attention?

If we look back to the odious examples of the past we are confronted by Adolf Hitler and Josef Stalin, both virulently anti-Semitic, and both of whom waged war against identifiable groups in their own countries.

Hitler was more selective, but both he and Stalin, who also included people of the Jewish faith in his "purges," directed their savagery at "enemies of the people," and contrived to kill, between them, and quite apart from war casualties, almost 64 million people (Hitler: 20,946,000; Stalin: 42,672,000).

Mao Tse-tung, another monster, was responsible for the deaths of some 35 millions of his own people. Pol Pot, in a much smaller country with far fewer people, contrived to slaughter about one-third of Cambodia's population.[3]

This illustrates the danger of applying labels to communism or fascism or socialism. All are manifestations of the political left, of state management of the economy, and the resulting coercion and conflict.

An American scholar has pointed out that communism and fascism were rival brands of socialism. Communism, or Marxist socialism, was founded on the idea of an international class struggle while fascist national socialism embraced socialism that focused on national unity. Both communists and fascists opposed the bourgeoisie; both attacked the conservatives and both were mass movements. Both favoured strong, centralized governments; both rejected a free economy and the ideals of individual liberty.

It was the official Marxist definition of fascism that assigned it to the right wing of politics by defining fascism as Marxism's polar opposite. Therefore, if Marxism was progressive, fascism must be conservative. If Marxism was socialist, fascism must be capitalist.[4]

Yet, to the very end of the Third Reich, Hitler's *National-Sozialistiche-Deutsche-Arbeiter-Partei* "proudly advertised itself as both a 'socialist' and a 'workers' party' in order to emphasize its popularity with the labouring masses of Germany."[5]

British historian Paul Johnson wrote that far from big business corrupting Hitler's socialism, it was the other way around.

Like Mussolini before him, and whom he much admired ("Everything within the state, nothing outside the state, nothing against the state" Mussolini boasted), it didn't matter to Hitler who owned the factories so long as the managers did what the state told them to do. Hitler thought that Lenin's worst mistake was to substitute party members for industry's capitalist managers.[6]

The political right, castigated by Canada's media as "reactionary," rejects state coercion in favour of a free market economy wherein participants are free to act in their own interests, provided they do not restrict or in any way infringe upon the freedom of others to do the same.

The reader may say, Ah! but those monsters of the past were dictators. Yes they were, after they had consolidated their power. But all of them were in the business of social engineering, and on their way to power they were much admired by the intelligentsia.

Mussolini had "an astonishing number of intellectual followers, by no means all of them Italian." In Hitler's rise to power, consistently he "was most successful on the campus." Stalin had "legions of intellectual admirers in his time, as did such post-war men of violence as Castro, Nasser and Mao Tse-tung."[7]

In our journey through the stages by which Quebec-dominated federal governments have chipped away at national morale, let us examine the effect of adding the Hate Propaganda section to Canada's Criminal Code as illustrated by a study of the press reports during the period 1970 to 1994.

The study was undertaken by Barbara Kulaszka[8], and it covered forty-four instances of alleged infractions contrary to section 319 (2) above; namely, "communicating statements, other than in private conversation, [that] wilfully promotes hatred against any identifiable group."

It surveyed press reports of "high-profile" allegations that reached the national media, and excluded complaints made to police that were not reported by the media.

In her conclusions, Ms. Kulaszka noted that high-profile public accusations of "hatred" were made by two main groups, ethnic lobbies and politicians, "but there is an extremely low ratio between the number of accusations and the number of charges laid."

Lest citizens take comfort from this, she adds the caveat: "The accusations have the effect of controlling the boundaries of acceptable public opinion and of stifling dissent from government policies such as official bilingualism and multiculturalism."

In that sentence is contained the proof of the pudding that Pierre Trudeau cooked for us:

- First the language laws that antagonized the country's majority.

- Then the multicultural policy that was designed to disintegrate the Canadian majority and hoodwink it into swallowing bilingualism.

- Then the radically changed written constitution that "entrenched" the linguistic and multicult industries in finicky legalese that no one could understand.

- All of this leading to the "fifty years of dissent" that Bora Laskin predicted and which the hate laws are now in place to suffocate.

In a letter to me, Ms. Kulaszka said she "spoke to some of the people mentioned in the study and the only word to describe their reaction to what happened to them is 'terror.' They could not believe that what they had written or said had nearly destroyed their lives."

Hate laws have no place in a liberal society. They are weapons in the hands not of the people but of the Thought Police who would rule the people.

No one should be surprised by Ms. Kulaszka's remark that throughout the twenty-four years her report covered:

The very small number of criminal charges and/or bannings have been of persons who are politically active in extreme right-wing organizations such as the Western Guard, the Nationalist Party, the Heritage Front, the Ku Klux Klan and WAR. No similar attention has been paid to the extreme left-wing of the political spectrum.

The fact that the study was confined to allegations that reached the national media, and the other fact that left-wing activities went unremarked, remind us of the left-wing tilt of the Canadian media as a whole.

In a typical example, on August 9, 1995, Susan Delacourt of *The Globe and Mail's* Parliamentary Bureau wrote about Progressive Conservative leader Jean Charest's search for a political platform. In her article she described the political stances of the Conservative premiers in Alberta and Ontario as "hard-right." Yet they comprised such propositions as "keeping taxes down," "making government smaller," "putting young people to work or training programs in exchange for their social benefits," "the idea of a flat tax aimed at simplifying the system," and "policies that encourage people to look to themselves, not government, to create a caring society."

Search the pages of the *Globe*, the *Toronto Star*, the *Toronto Sun*, *Saturday Night* and *Maclean's* magazines, and you will not find a single reference, year in, year out, to a politician or a party or a political stance as "hard-left."

The policies and practices of the Pearson/Trudeau years, prolonged almost unchanged through the years of Brian Mulroney and Jean Chrétien, have so accustomed Canada's journalists to the left-wing politics that marked those thirty years that they are regarded as occupying the political centre.

Official bilingualism and multiculturalism, affirmative action programs, redistribution of incomes and tax revenues between individuals and regions, equalization of outcomes, "progressive" income tax, banding of public servants into labour unions with the right to strike, proliferation of commissions and committees and tribunals with arbitrary powers - the whole panoply of state intrusion into the private lives of the citizens has become so ingrained as to be accepted as the norm in Canadian society.

The great truth to which, with a few honourable exceptions, Canadian journalists and commentators and writers and dramatists are not so much wilfully as unconsciously blind, is that the country's economic and political ills are the inevitable result of thirty years of socialism.

A paternalistic state, which socialists portray in a golden light of peaceful contentment whence want has been banished and where needs are fulfilled, is indeed utopian: it exists only in fancy or theory.

That this is so needs only the proof of socialist experiments worldwide that have suffered at best insolvency; at worst, the horrors unleashed by demented dictators.

The error lies in a prideful belief in the perfectibility of mankind, always provided that people can be made to follow the precepts laid down by their guardians. Thus does socialism *always* lead to coercion.

The leftward tilt of the Pearson-Trudeau years found further expression in the attitude of Canadian publishers toward opposing views. From my own experience I can testify to the difficulty, amounting to effective censorship, of getting any such work published. In the early 1970s, when it had become obvious that publishers who were on the receiving end of government subsidies were not about to bite the hand that fed them, I had the good fortune to meet Winnett Boyd, the brilliant Canadian engineer and inventor who designed Canada's first jet engine and also the world's first nuclear research facility at Chalk River, Ontario.

Winn was then running the Canadian operation of Arthur D. Little, the well-known American firm of consulting engineers, but he was also a strong advocate of Louis Kelso's ideas for widespread capital ownership that were taking root through Employee Share Ownership Plans (ESOPs).

I had written *Red Maple*, in which with Winn's help ESOP ideas were included, and which among other things forecast (seven years before the event) Pierre Trudeau's overthrow of Canada's common law tradition and its replacement with the state-directed Quebec model in a written constitution. None of the subsidized publishers would touch it. At McClelland & Stewart, "The Canadian Publishers," I was told that "our younger readers didn't like it - too radical"; no doubt a reflection of what they were being taught in schools and colleges.

Together Winn and I wrote a book, *The National Dilemma, And The Way Out*, which showed how all three federal parties were committed to socialistic policies and that the answer lay in a widespread diffusion of capital ownership as a development of the ESOP principle. This too was rejected out of hand by leading publishers. Jack McClelland perked up a bit when Winn offered to guarantee the first 5,000 sales, but we could tell he didn't want to go with it and after we left we saw no reason why we too should subsidize his overhead.

We formed BMG Publishing Limited strictly on sweat equity and between 1975 and 1979 we published eight titles. All were by authors whose work had been rejected by the subsidized publishers, all sold more than 10,000 copies, and all were on popular topics - Pierre Trudeau's commitment to socialism; radical changes to immigration; multiculturalism; the planned spread of French power through official bilingualism; and the need to quell the growth of the state - which other publishers were afraid to tackle. Jock Andrew's *Bilingual Today, French Tomorrow*, a prescient look at Pierre Trudeau's revolution, was a runaway bestseller that survived orchestrated attempts to suppress it, including pressure on Coles bookstore by a Liberal senator, to reach a final total of 130,000 sold.

For years after we closed BMG I was still getting manuscripts from frustrated authors who had been through the same runaround as BMG's writers. In 1989 I wrote *Keeping Canada Together*, met the same rejections as before, joined with a friend, Bill Bolt, to publish it under the name of his business systems company, and we sold two printings of 3,000 each.

This little essay - a personal experience of Barbara Kulaska's observation about stifling dissent from government policies - is a tiny illustration of a very large matter: no less than the crushing of free speech in Canada. Those fine words in Mr. Trudeau's Charter "guaranteeing" that everyone has freedom of thought, belief, opinion and expression, including freedom of the press and other media of communication, are not worth the paper they are printed on; the ever-intrusive state has other ways of denying the freedom it "guarantees."

Today as I write, the *Globe* describes how a former MLA and cabinet minister in British Columbia was fired from cabinet, resigned his seat, was hounded by the press and became unemployable after allegations of sexual harassment were made anonymously to the reporters who turned them into headlines. Later, two women "went public" with complaints to the BC Human Rights Commission, which covered any legal costs they might incur. But the man incurred personal legal costs of $60,000 and a ruined life that brought suffering to his wife and children. For three years he was denied entry to a court of law, but even when the BC Court of Appeal dismissed the human rights case on the grounds of justice delayed, the BC Human Rights Commission appealed the decision and was seeking leave to have the case heard by the Supreme Court of Canada.

Much of the foregoing, I suggest, is an inevitable outcome of the Trudeau coup de force (Robert Stanfield called it a coup d'état). The 1981-82 exercise in deception that achieved the life-long goal of its author was by its nature revolutionary.

It overthrew a tradition of inherent freedom that had evolved and been fought for through the generations since Anglo-Saxon times, and substituted a system that is now revealed by its practices; namely, one in which rights and freedoms are limited by definitions, bypassed by commissions and tribunals with arbitrary powers, and interpreted by unelected judges beyond the reach of Parliament to afford means of redress.

By favouring groups - the collective - over the individual, it fosters dissent.

The thrust to centralize power in the hands of a few originates from the power that is centred in the office of prime minister, power that has increased since the revolution and that runs counter to Canada's democratic tradition.

On August 25, 1996, responding to a call from a provincial premiers' conference to give provinces a larger role in running social programs, in short to recover some of the power that had been theirs exclusively before the revolution, Prime Minister Jean Chrétien said that Ottawa would continue to enforce national standards by withholding money from provinces that contravened the standards.

Since Jean Chrétien was Pierre Trudeau's left-hand man in the 1982 deception; since he is wedded to the French style of centralized authority that the Charter imposed; since a divided Opposition secured his re-election in 1997 for a second term; and since his likely successor is also from Quebec, no relief is in sight from the Canadian paradox.

To repeat, just as the French tradition predisposes Quebecers to centralized authority within the province, so must they resist attempts by the federal government to invade their provincial government's constitutional territory.

Their political acumen enables them to vote strategically in federal elections, assuring them of enough political power to get material benefits from Ottawa. Yet their adherence to the original Constitution's division of powers prompts them to resist the federal intrusions that redistribution entails.

At the same time a Quebec-dominated Liberal government in Ottawa, committed to centralized authority and to the redistribution of wealth and income that is required by the Charter, naturally favours the Quebec which, until the advent of the Mulroney Tories and the Bloc Québécois, formed its core support.

In 1998 the paradox was reconfirmed. When all ten provincial premiers had agreed that the federal spending power over social policy should be limited and that an impartial mechanism should be set up to settle disputes, Prime Minister Jean Chrétien rejected their proposals out of hand.

I conclude that the paradox cannot be resolved within the present political structure. When two levels of government insist on paramountcy in the same field, no compromise is possible.

When we consider that the centralized structure was imposed by a trick, that it represents the political convictions of at most 25 percent of Canada's population, and that the remaining 75 percent is heir to the contrary structure of inherent freedom and parliamentary supremacy under the evolving common law, then it is clear that the majority which inherited the contrary structure must find some means of reinstating it.

Here the reader might ask what the Charter has to do with the growth of the state, and it is therefore appropriate to spend a few moments in examining its provisions.

As befits a product of committees, the Charter begins with a contradiction. Having declared that Canada is founded upon principles that recognize the supremacy of God and the rule of law, the Charter contrives not to mention God again and to concern itself solely with the works of man, while casting doubt on its commitment to the rule of law.

It arrogates to itself the power to guarantee certain rights and freedoms, subject only to such reasonable limits prescribed by law as can be demonstrably justified in a free and democratic society, whose freedom it then proceeds to circumscribe with conditions.

As a natural consequence of the judiciary's elevation to supreme authority, judges were to start making law as well as interpreting it.

In a 1981 article Madam Justice Rosalie Abella saw a strong role for judges in making new law when the occasion demanded. "Is there a role for the court as the conscience of the community, giving expression to ideas as a means of educating and directing society's thoughts?" Her answer: "In family law, more than any other area of law, the courts and legislature are 'partners in the enterprise of lawmaking.'"[9]

Judge Abella, who served as a one-woman royal commission on equality in 1984, wrote a report that led to the 1986 federal employment equity law, and coined the term "employment equity" to replace the Charter's definition of "affirmative action."

She also wrote "Equality demands enforcement." It was not enough to be able to claim equal rights unless they were enforceable.[10]

The Charter enumerates, in considerable detail, and again subject to conditions, a variety of rights that Canadians are entitled to: democratic, mobility, legal, equality, and linguistic.

Missing from the catalogue is Canadians' right to the private ownership of property.

While that right could be regarded as contained within the common law, the fact that it was expressly excluded from the Charter at the instance of the officially socialist New Democratic Party, is significant.

It is of a piece with the outlook displayed by Supreme Court Chief Justice Dickson in 1986 that the court "must be guided by the values and principles essential to a free and democratic society."

These included "commitment to social justice and equality" and "social and political institutions which enhance the participation of individuals and groups in society."[11]

There is also a contradiction between recognizing the rule of law and then asserting that the law will be used to discriminate against different kinds of people who are declared at the same time to be equal before and under the law.

The Charter is now Canada's supreme law (Section 52.1).

Madam Justice Abella's attribution to judges of a strong role in making new law when the occasion demands, former Chief Justice Dickson's committing the court to social justice and equality and to institutions that enhance the participation of individuals and groups in society - couple these declarations with the virtual powerlessness of individual Canadians, as we shall see in the next chapter, to seek redress through the courts, and we are faced with a constitutional commitment to the growth of the state.

Moreover, since judges now have a strong role in making new law, since the common law is to be brought into line with the near-unamendable decrees of the Charter, and since judges are as susceptible to differing political opinions as anyone else, whatever opinions they bring to the task are likely to be as unrepresentative of the people, as expressed in Parliament, as are the judges themselves.

This too is a cause of dissent.

The state's growth began with the gradual insertion of socialism under Pearson and Trudeau, took its big jump with the fraudulent imposition of the Charter, and has bequeathed to judges the Herculean task of deciphering and lending substance to the Charter's obscurities - what University of Toronto Professor Peter Russell called "limp balloons which the constitution makers handed to the judiciary; the judges must now decide how much air to blow into them."[12]

What they are unlikely to blow into them, we might conclude from the judges' observations on the matter, is a breath of the word of God. The Charter, like the socialism that inspired its concoction, is wholly secular.

Not only is the Charter's declared supremacy a radical departure from Canada's tradition of parliamentary sovereignty; it is also a departure from Judeo-Christian principles embedded in the evolving common law that until 1982 was the framework of Canada's social order.

While it is true that the criminal code proscribes certain acts and describes the penalties for committing them - the 1999 edition of *Martin's Criminal Code* contains some 2,000 pages of things that Canadians can be fined or imprisoned for doing - the Charter concerns itself with Canadians' entitlements and what they are *permitted* to do provided there aren't any laws, programs or activities that might interfere with their trying to do them.

By contrast, the common law is a body of general rules prescribing social conduct that has developed over centuries from decisions reached by juries and judges in particular cases brought before the courts. Clearly it is man-made law, but just as clearly it is consistent with the prescriptions that God handed down to Moses and which were later interpreted by Jesus.

All of the prescriptions were spiritual matters. It was up to the people as individuals to make their own decisions; either to follow the rules or to break them.

Between the two concepts is an unbridgeable gap: on one side the paternalistic state telling people what they are entitled to; on the other a set of rules for behaviour and the God-given freedom to follow them or not.

To put the difference another way: under the civil code what is not allowed is forbidden; under the common law that has developed since Anglo-Saxon times what is not forbidden is allowed.

Former Chief Justice Dickson's committing the courts to "social justice and equality" and "social and political institutions which enhance the participation of individuals and groups in society" both involve coercion.

Social justice is jargon for redistributing wealth from people who created it, or created more of it, to other people who didn't create so much or created none at all. Quite separate, and different in kind, from the charity that people practice of their own volition, it is a corruption of the rule of law by government that is supposed to uphold it; in other words it is an action not by government but by the state.

Linking "equality" to "social justice" compounds the corruption, while declaring that "equality demands enforcement" gives the socialist game away: the "equality" of "social justice" is incompatible with liberty.

At first glance, "social and political institutions which enhance the participation of individuals and groups in society" might be taken as including such voluntary institutions as churches or service clubs - until we realize that the courts have nothing to do with voluntary institutions.

Courts came into play the moment the Charter demanded "amelioration" of the conditions of people who are "socially or economically disadvantaged" or who are disadvantaged because of race, national or ethnic origin, colour, religion, sex, age or mental or physical disability.

If they are disadvantaged because of age, mental or physical disability, they fall within the category of people that most Canadians would agree to help through the agency of government. But to what extent, if at all, the condition of all the others should be ameliorated is clearly debatable.

Until 1982, such a debate would have been confined to Parliament, and the outcome would have entered the statutes where it would be open to amendment or repeal by later parliaments. But now it is ordained by Canada's supreme law that an indeterminate number of individuals who consider themselves disadvantaged for a variety of reasons are entitled to have their conditions "ameliorated." No longer is it a matter of entitlement; that has been decided. It is now a matter of degree, which only the courts can decide.

Similarly with the requirement that the Charter be interpreted in a manner consistent with the preservation and enhancement of Canada's multicultural heritage (Section 27).

This involves the law in any dispute about the sources and categories of immigrants; if not through the regular courts then through one or another of the state's tribunals and commissions established for the purpose.

A court, the dictionary tells us, is a place where justice is judicially administered. Justice is the quality of being judged; the rendering of what is due or merited. It also implies a strict rendering of deserts. More narrowly, to administer justice means to apply the law of the land.

The Charter is Canada's supreme law. It entitles every individual not only to the equal protection but to the equal *benefit* of the law which is required to ameliorate the condition of certain individuals and to enhance Canada's condition of multiculturalism.

These activities, of benefitting, ameliorating and enhancing, are positive. They require the law-applying agencies; that is, the courts, tribunals and commissions, to do things. The benefits, ameliorations and enhancements are all additives to the natural condition of the individuals to whom they are applied. Since they are applied by courts which have no resources save the power of the law, and since the individuals are not contending against other individuals who might be charged the resulting costs, if the courts are to render what is due or merited they must render any resulting costs from somewhere outside the courts.

That "somewhere" is the state and the funds the state either extracts from the citizens or borrows on their credit.

This brings us back to Justice Dickson's social and political institutions which enhance the participation of individuals and groups in society.

Unlike voluntary institutions, whose independence consists in their means of support (volunteers, and money freely given from supporters' after-tax income), the social and political institutions known generally as advocacy groups, and which are funded wholly or in part by the state, had grown to such an extent by 1993 as to fill 102 pages of the Secretary of State's section of the public accounts.

These are the groups whose staffs exemplify the distinction between government as referee and the state as player. It is they who have the time - because the state funds them for the purpose - to badger the state's commissions and tribunals for favours.

Moreover, that misuse of public funds is aggravated when the governing party co-opts the groups to serve partisan ends.

Authorizing grants and subsidies to advocacy groups is a political matter. The governing party attracts appeals from, and is sympathetic to, groups espousing claims or policies that it agrees with.

By this means, it recruits an underground of vocal support that serves as a continual focus for print and electronic journalists seeking "spokespersons" on events of the day. Thus is the governing party's bias reinforced not only by the conjunction of its favoured - and funded - groups with the media, but also by inserting a body of favourable opinion into the populace that responds to pollsters.

Furthermore, the state's commissions and tribunals, whose intrusions into our personal lives are perennial generators of news, and whose staffs have ready access to the media, are at pains to lend vocal and written support to the governing party's policies at every opportunity.

CRTC Chairman Keith Spicer declared that he would use his authority to "keep pushing" social and cultural goals by "pressing the market" and "considering regulation only when all else fails."[13]

All of this contributes to the growth of the state at the expense of individual freedom. As the state intrudes into our personal lives, so does it compress that part of them in which we are free to decide for ourselves.

It does this in two ways: first by taking away increasing proportions of our money so that we have less to spend or save; and second by distributing some of it among people and causes that are the concerns not of government but of partisan politics.

Once begun, an inclination to rely upon the state is bound to accelerate under the influence of the human tendency to do the easier things first and to put off the harder ones indefinitely.

The number of easier things is limited only by the imagination and ingenuity of the civil servants and commentators who propose that they be dealt with. When they have a ready made instruction manual in the form of the country's supreme law, the task falls into tidy compartments that are identified by the Charter.

These boil down to (first) securing and spreading the French language, and (second) controlling as much of the economy and the rights and entitlements of the citizens as are consistent with a paternalistic welfare state.

When the state sets out to equalize the different, it encourages dissension by persuading some people that they are more different than the general run and that they should be compensated for the difference.

The authority for this is Section 15 of the Charter which says that everyone has the right to equal benefit of the law without discrimination based on race, national or ethnic origin, colour, religion, sex, age or mental or physical disability; but that none of this prevents the state from stepping in to ameliorate the conditions of people who are disadvantaged for any of those reasons.

This does three things:

- **First**, it draws attention to the existence of different groups which the Charter also identifies by defining them - by race, nationality, ethnic origin and so on.
- **Second**, it discriminates in favour of those defined groups at the expense of the majority which adheres to the British tradition of *everyone's* enjoyment of inherent freedom under the common law.

- **Third**, the definitions and discriminations fit snugly into the state's prohibitions about spreading hatred against these same identifiable groups.

In sum, the state creates multiculturalism by diverting immigration away from traditional sources. But instead of letting everyone adjust to the change at their own pace, the state assumes the worst and introduces hate laws to punish people who speak out against the policy.

The enforcement of equality made its way through parliamentary committees to entry in the statutes as the Employment Equity Act (1986). From there it moved into an Interdepartmental Working Group on Employment Equity Data which set about defining visible minorities according to certain criteria. These were incorporated in the Census.

Thus questions 13 through 21 of the 1996 Census were described as providing "a social and cultural profile of Canada's population."

They asked where people were born, of what country they were citizens, if they were landed immigrants and if so since what year, which ethnic group they belonged to (French, English, German, Scottish, Canadian, Italian, Irish, Chinese, Cree, Micmac, Métis, Inuit {Eskimo}, Ukrainian, Dutch, East Indian, Polish, Portuguese, Jewish, Haitian, Jamaican, Vietnamese, Lebanese, Chilean, Somali, etc.).

Then respondents were asked whether they were aboriginal, a member of an Indian Band/First Nation, or a Treaty Indian, or White, Chinese, South Asian, Black, Arab/West Indian, Latin American, Japanese, Korean or other.

The purpose, the accompanying guide explained, was to track population movements, to determine the number of potential voters, to compare socio-economic conditions of immigrants over time, to assist reviews of immigration and employment policies and programs, as well as to plan education, health, and other services.

But the crux of it was in regard to the questions about ethnic or cultural groups (Italian, Irish, Cree, etc.) and race (White, Black, Chinese, etc.).

These were to provide information "required under the Multiculturalism Act and the Canadian Charter of Rights and Freedoms...information used extensively by ethnic or cultural associations, government agencies and researchers for a wide range of activities such as health promotion, communications and marketing." Also to provide information "about the visible minority population in Canada required for programs under the Employment Equity Act, which promotes equal opportunity for everyone."

The first census taken after passage of the Employment Equity Act was in 1991 and four years later, in its summer 1995 issue of *Canadian Social Trends*, Statistics Canada published an analysis by staff member Karen Kelly of what was happening to visible minorities.[14]

The analysis revealed a number of similarities. Visible minorities tended to concentrate in Canada's larger cities, accounting for 24 percent of the adult population in Toronto, 23 percent in Vancouver, and 10 percent in Montreal, and almost all of them lived in urban areas.

They were generally more highly educated than other adults yet were somewhat less likely to be employed in professional or managerial jobs. Many were concentrated in lower-paying clerical, service and manual labour jobs.

Different groups favoured different cities. Toronto attracted 50 percent of Blacks and Koreans, 48 percent of South Asians, and 42 percent of Filipinos. Almost half of the Pacific Islanders (49 percent) were in Vancouver.

Chinese and Japanese were split between Toronto (39 percent and 27 percent, respectively) and Vancouver (28 percent and 31 percent).

Montreal attracted 35 percent of West Asians, 24 percent of Latin Americans and Arabs and 20 percent of Blacks.

Within the groups there was considerable difference in education. Highest with university degrees were Koreans (36 percent), Japanese and West Asians and Arabs (28 percent each) and Filipinos (26 percent). Lowest were Pacific Islanders (9 percent), Black (13 percent), Latin Americans (14 percent), and South East Asians (16 percent).

Men and women in these groups were of similar proportions, women slightly lower than men.

From the numerous tables in the report, and after proportions had been "age-standardized" to provide a comparison with other adults, one thing stood out: unless immigration policies are changed, Canada's visible minority population will continue to diversify, and the state's intrusions under the authorities of the Multiculturalism Act and the Employment Equity Act will continue to grow.

In the employment stakes, some groups do better than others.

Chinese, Koreans, Filipinos, Pacific Islanders, and Japanese show unemployment rates at or below the Canadian average. Latin Americans, South East Asians, West Asians and Arabs, South Asians, and Blacks show rates higher than the average. Yet after "age-standardization," visible minorities as a whole show an unemployment rate only 3 percent higher than other adults.

In another part of the same publication, we find that immigrants as a whole, both men and women, were more likely to be self-employed than were those Canadians who were born here. This applied at all ages and across all industries.

When we review the sequence of events that led to this orgy of head-counting and classification, we are confronted once again with the ugly face of politics.

Priority for the radicals from Quebec was to protect the language laws from repeal. With that achieved by the "patriation" deception, they could move on to consolidate political gains from the Charter's parallel imposition of multiculturalism.

At first, multiculturalism had been a device to divert attention from the divisive effects of the "two founding races" myth and its offshoots in two languages and two cultures. By establishing "a policy of multiculturalism within a bilingual framework" the radicals hoped to placate the one-third of Canadians whose origins were neither English nor French.

But then it was only natural to build on the 180 degree change in immigration rules that was concocted in 1967 when the Liberals discovered that some thirty federal ridings, chiefly in Ontario, were being decided by less than 500 votes. Accordingly, they changed the rules in favour of immigrants from the Third World, many of whom vote gratefully for the Liberals.

Ten years later, columnist and former MP Douglas Fisher wrote that anyone reading the immigration data for the decade would "understand why the Liberals advocate multiculturalism so strongly."

Later still, when "enhancing" multiculturalism had been entrenched in the Charter, those thirty-odd ridings that would be forever Liberal could be joined by others in Montreal and Vancouver courtesy of the affirmative action provisions of the Charter, the Employment Equity Act of 1986, and future electoral successes fertilized every five years by the census.

Between them, the Trudeau Liberals, the Mulroney Conservatives who succeeded them, and the Chrétien Liberals who took power in 1993 have been in the business of importing new voters all the time, and in numbers 2.5 times greater per capita of population than immigrants to the USA. Since many are attracted to Canada by "universal" social programs that kick in for immigrants the moment they set foot at a Canadian airport, governments automatically strengthen the grip of the welfare state with every planeload.

While all this was being engineered, however, the minority that formerly was known as French Canadian adroitly insulated itself from the classification process by assuming the generic title of Québécois so that it could move step by step into the sovereignty that the new name implied.

In later chapters I shall suggest that an apparent decline in the morale of Canada's armed forces reflects a decline in the morale of the Canadian *nation* they are sworn to defend. Here, in the matter of enlisting immigrants to vote for a political party, we are reminded of the obsession that drove Pierre Trudeau to impose multiculturalism and to embody its divisive requirements in the Charter.

The obsession was his "consuming aversion" to Quebec nationalism.[15] It arose from his long-held view that nations belonged "to a transitional period in world history" - a view he shared with his predecessor. At the 1968 Couchiching Conference, Lester Pearson urged Canadians to work to create a new kind of internationalism rather than trying to reinforce national independence.

When we are also reminded that Canada's armed forces are recruited and sworn to serve in the defence of the *Canadian* nation, we are entitled to ask by what right does the Government of Canada persist in encouraging immigrants to perpetuate their links with the nations they came from?

One purpose, we can understand, is the venal one of the natural governing party to garner votes, but when we make the connection with that party's fostering of dissent, and of its neglect of the armed forces which are government's ultimate resource in enforcing the law, it is hard to avoid the conclusion that the whole endeavour is aimed at weakening Canadians' sense of nationhood so that they can fit into this transitional period in world history.

It is also one more example of the split between instincts of partisan politicians and those of the Canadians they are supposed to represent. Given half a chance, Canadians of whatever origin, language or colour will do their level best to get along with one another. This does not mean that they will seek out people who are manifestly different. Everyone exercises preferences. Everyone is comfortable with people who share their tastes within the endless variety of which a nation consists.

Nor does it mean that people will go out of their way to patronize others who appear to be different. Recognizing any such attempt as both rude and intrusive, they will leave them alone unless they are asked for help, in which event Canadians take second place to none in their readiness to respond, and generously.

The split is between the preferences of men and women as independent individuals, and the preferences of the paternalistic state as personified by certain politicians and public servants.

The former choose their friends, and associate voluntarily with others; the latter would force everyone to obey rules and procedures which classify people and accord some of them special treatment. In the words of the learned judge: "Equality demands enforcement." As we remarked before, socialism *always* involves coercion.

Statistics have their uses, but the moment they are corrupted for political purposes, they become powerful tools of the intrusive state. The fact that many members of visible minorities "were concentrated in lower-paying clerical, service and manual labour jobs" invites a host of state-funded agencies to spring into action: the respective "ethnic" groups; "race-relations" groups; MPs, MPPs, and local councillors of a left-liberal persuasion; and the Pay Equity Commission itself.

Ignored by all those busybodies are two salient facts: everyone is different from everyone else; and, except for special cases of the rich and independent, all immigrants traditionally expected to start near the bottom, to prove their worth, and to progress accordingly.

Many of them still do, but many others are lured to Canada by state-inspired promotion of the handouts that await them the moment they set foot from the aircraft onto Canadian soil.

In that deceitful use of public funds, again for political purposes, great harm is done to the Canadian polity, for it spreads among immigrants at a most impressionable time the vision, not of progress through their individual efforts, but of a future secured by the bountiful Canadian state.

Since the bountiful Canadian state followed the course of other socialist utopias into insolvency, and since actions by the governing Liberals to offload the ensuing debt to provincial governments are causing hardship to society's most vulnerable citizens, it will be appropriate to devote the next two chapters to contributory factors.

First is the business initiative that creates Canada's wealth, and how that initiative is stunted by the state's interference by means of its allies the courts and labour unions.

Second is the matter of the state's revenue-chasing, in which our absurdly complex tax system has been consistently counter-productive.

Chapter 3

Civil order threatened

Socialism's enduring fallacy lies in a misunderstanding of this life that we live every day, and in which we are changing all the time. The influences that change us - other people, new ideas, age and time - are infinitely variable and we tackle them as best we can, but the fact that they are there is a condition of our lives.

Thus the daily struggle of a business enterprise to create wealth is a magnification of life itself. The influences are stronger because opposing entrepreneurs are trying their best to out-produce, or out-sell, or out-innovate our own best efforts. But they too are defending themselves against assaults of ours in a continual contest.

Ideally, it would take place on a level field that in fact is never flat. The competition that stimulates both enterprise and economy of effort is eroded by a number of factors; some due to combinations of other businesses or of labour unions, some to the state's intrusions by means of taxes, tariffs and regulations, some to government's failure to exercise its legitimate power.

All of these reflect people's natural instincts to find short cuts, to make life easier for themselves, and to increase their share of whatever wealth is being created.

But just as government uses its legitimate power to prevent us from harming one another's persons, property, or reputations, so should it use that power, of which it is granted a monopoly, to prohibit the citizens from forming monopolies of their own.

In the world of business, monopoly is sometimes mistaken for competitive advantage. At a cross-roads, far from the nearest village, a country store has the advantage that derives from convenience. Its customers weigh the advantages of proximity, or neighbourliness, or of its being open most of the time, against the fact of higher prices that the store must charge to cover its costs.

In towns and cities, "convenience" stores make their livelihoods on similar grounds. None of these is in restraint of trade. All of them are subject to competition.

A fledgling company that looks to another company for services it cannot afford on its own - domestic marketing or foreign sales - is no more in restraint of trade than is the company that provides the services.

Even very large and powerful corporations, which might appear on the surface to be monopolistic because of their size and share of the markets for what they make and sell, even they are subject to competition from others equally large.

Chrysler, Ford, and General Motors; Labatts and Molsons; Esso and Gulf and Shell; IBM and Texas Instruments and Microsoft - despite their apparent dominance, even these giants are vulnerable to time and chance. Of the 25 largest US corporations in 1917, only 13 were on the list in 1957; only 7 made it to the 1986 list.[1]

It is when large corporations become involved with other powerful forces that an economy suffers effects similar to those of monopoly. Those forces are labour unions and the state.

A labour union is an association of workers organized to improve working conditions and advance mutual interests.

From that apparently innocent intention has grown a variety of associations whose mutual interests are defined less by the welfare of the associated workers than by political aspirations of the unions' leaders.

Their aspirations are rarely toward competing for political office; rather do they seek the prominence, bolstered by the attention of journalists who also are union members, that enables them to influence the political class.

That class in turn, driven as always by hunger for votes, sees a greater benefit from pandering to the many, represented by union leaders, than from pandering to the relatively few corporate executives who employ them.

They of the business class are looked to for funding rather than votes, funding that looks, again in turn, to the state for political rewards. These are made possible by the exercise of political power in such matters as:

- favourable treatment in bids for state-funded contracts;
- favourable restraint of trade through federal or provincial regulation;
- review and possible change of some other regulation;
- favourable interpretation of provisions affecting tariffs, duties or taxes.

This trinity of interests - corporations, union leaders, and politicians - runs counter to the interests not only of the people in general but also of the particular people the corporations and unions are supposed to serve.

The shareholders who are at least the nominal owners of the corporations suffer from the state's intrusion into corporate affairs that outweighs any temporary advantage pried from the political class.

The union members suffer loss of freedom through forced membership in, and payment of dues to unions which use part of those dues to support causes they might not agree with, while being conscripted periodically into strikes that have more to do with asserting the power of the union's leaders than with the members' own well-being.

The whole effect of the combination is to enlarge the role of the state to which both corporations and unions look for competitive advantage that amounts to restraint of trade.

Corporate power derives from the state and is a function both of politics and of an absurdly complex, and dangerously counterproductive, tax system that will be treated in the next chapter.

But union power is also reinforced by court rulings, and because of the union movement's negative effect upon employment in Canada - another cause of dissent - it is worth reviewing what some of the courts have done.

Union power owes much to the settlement arrived at in January 1946 by Mr. Justice Ivan Rand of the Supreme Court of Canada to end a bitter four-month strike against the Ford company in the Ontario city of Windsor.

Both parties accepted an award, known as the Rand Formula, that denied the unions' request for a union shop; instead it required all workers covered by the collective agreement to pay union dues whether they belonged to the union or not.

The award also provided for penalties against individuals engaging in wildcat strikes, and against a union that called a strike without authorization by a secret ballot of all employees.

The Rand Formula required that no strike would be called without a vote by government-supervised secret ballot of all employees covered by the agreement.

The union would repudiate any illegal or unauthorized strike and declare any picket line supporting such a strike to be illegal and not binding on its members. Any employee participating in such a strike would lose one year of seniority for every week, or part thereof, of absence from work and be fined (1946) $3 per day.

A union failing to repudiate such a strike would lose all right to the dues check-off for a period varying from two to six months. After 10 months from the start of the (compulsory dues check-off) agreement, 25 percent of the employees could demand a secret ballot under government supervision to determine if the union would continue as the employees' bargaining agent.[2]

Yet the only survivor of this balance of concessions and penalties was compulsory unionism with its built-in guarantee of a permanent source of union funds to which all employees were compelled by law to contribute; in effect, a union monopoly of labour and a denial of the workers' freedom of association.

Now it is true that advances in telecommunications and computer technology are reducing the power of the corporate-union-state interface.

As industry tends toward diffusion and dispersal, so does the organization of workers into unions become more difficult. But while this is happening, the growth of the state continues, not so much in the numbers of people it employs - for debt recovery dictates some reduction in the numbers - as in the influence it exerts on widening circles of its dependents.

Leading that congregation of interests are the "public service" labour unions that have been formed from employees of the state and who constitute a declining union movement's residual strength.

Although union membership accounts for little more than one-third of the Canadian workforce, 85 percent of government employees are unionized. (This represents a major difference between Canada and its largest market and competitor, the United States, where the overall rate of union membership is about 15 percent, split between private sector, 10 percent, and public sector, 37 percent.)

Here it is appropriate to recall the circumstances of the Dominion government's employees before then prime minister Lester Pearson gave them the right to strike.

Canada's civil service, which was justifiably credited with the healthy condition of public finance after the Dominion's magnificent contribution to, and huge expenditure on, two world wars, enjoyed a reputation for competence and dedication that was second to none in the industrialized world.

Pay might be lower than its members could have earned in private employment, but this was offset by their employment's settled conditions: fixed and by no means onerous working hours, generous vacations, assurance of a job, and an adequate pension on retirement.

It was the Treasury Board's responsibility to oversee working conditions, including pay and allowances, as it was the responsibility of other civil servants in the various staff associations to make representations for change.

Both sides, Treasury Board representing the Dominion, and association members representing the staff, were composed of professionals who understood both the fiscal boundaries and the social implications of change.

In short, they were of a conservative disposition in the sense of inclining toward precedent and order, while admitting the legitimacy of liberal inclinations toward peaceful reform, all within a context of individual freedom under limited government: moderate people seeking compromise and consensus.

Into this civilized exchange was thrust the disruptive violence of the strike.

In the March 1977 edition of *The Labour Gazette*, the research director of the Canadian Union of Public Employees (Canada's largest union) wrote:

> Public employees in many jurisdictions are no longer content to keep pace with the private sector.
> A bright and more militant breed of younger public servants are determined to win conditions superior to those in the private sector. They are succeeding in many cases.

Their success depended on a number of factors. First was the strike itself, the use of force to prevent people from working, and the fact that the work they were duty-bound to do constituted one of government's monopolies in fields such as public education, transportation, air traffic control, and postal service where there was no competing entity to serve the public.

Second was the technique of the false comparison. By pointing to jobs in the private sector that appeared to be similar to jobs performed by civil servants, and which attracted higher pay, civil service unions demanded "parity" with the private sector.

This despite the marked difference in the two conditions of work: public work secure, with substantial benefits; private work insecure, with no or fewer benefits.

Third was the use of arbitrators to settle the strikes, and end the resulting deprivation of services to the public. The arbitrators would shuttle from one closed meeting to the other, arrive in due course at a compromise acceptable to both parties - all at the public expense -

and a precedent would be established for application across the board.

If, as inevitably happened, the pressure of monopoly enabled the civil service unions to "win" higher pay for particular job categories than was paid in the private sector, the corresponding private sector unions would themselves demand "parity" and the game of leapfrog would start again.

Nor was the damage confined to pay scales. Labour unions by their nature are coercive, dependent on the state's power to enforce their conditions of membership and collective action. "Collective bargaining" is a hallowed tenet of the union creed.

Their political home is the left wing of politics, especially the New Democratic Party of official socialists, but by no means unwelcome in the ranks of Progressive Conservatives and Liberals.

Consequently, the new militancy of public sector unions was reflected in administrative proposals it is the responsibility of civil servants to draft in their capacity as permanent advisers to governments of the day. The creation of social programs that outstripped governments' ability to pay for them owed much to the changing political inclination of the advisers.[3]

A by-product has been the accumulation of built-in disincentives to hiring that contributes to Canada's stubbornly high rate of unemployment.

In Ontario, for example, where the unemployment rate was about double the rate in neighbouring Michigan, the disincentives were formidable: payroll taxes, including unemployment insurance, workers' compensation and the employer health tax, plus the added expense of any company fringe benefits such as a dental plan, and wages determined not by market value but by scales set out in pay equity legislation.

If an employee was injured on the job, not only would the company face a possible increase in its workers' compensation assessment, it would also be required to take the employee back and guarantee work for up to two years.

If an employee became pregnant, she could not be laid off, even for cause.

If an employee was fired, the company would be faced not only with substantial severance payment but the likelihood of being hauled before an employment tribunal for unjust dismissal, or to the Human Rights Commission for "discriminatory" termination.

Pay equity legislation required companies to hire fixed percentages of employees according to government scales of race, gender and disability.

Noting that companies were obliged to hire staff for the sole purpose of dealing with the variety of taxes and regulations, *Toronto Star* columnist Howard Levitt wrote that "The issue is not whether these burdens are fair or reasonable. It is simply that many employers would prefer to avoid some of them. Some employers have even been put out of business or left Canada because of them."[4]

Union-inspired handicaps to entrepreneurship spring from the movement's militant origins ("picket" and "strike" are military terms), from its portrayal of "the bosses" as enemies, and from a continual quest for "victories" to justify the leaders' own jobs.

Between January 1989 and August 1993, factory-gate selling prices of manufactured goods rose 2.3 percent. In the same period, payroll taxes and supplementary benefits, imposed by governments, rose 43 percent. Regulated prices, controlled by governments, rose 23 percent.[5] In short, government as referee of competition had become the state as player.

This prostitution of government monopoly, while it illustrates the harmful effects of interaction between corporations, unions and the state, is exacerbated when it spills over into the small- and medium-sized enterprises that employ a majority of Canadians.

A large corporation can absorb union-forced pay and benefit rises partly because it has a large enough share of the market to dissipate the effect, but also because its competitors will be subjected to the same union pressure.

In a ritual long past due for abolition, the Canadian Auto Workers "selects" Chrysler, Ford or GM, for its routine assault. When a strike or the threat of one has produced the required improvements in pay and company-funded benefits, the union draws a bead on the other two corporations, the "improvements" are duly reflected in the prices of cars and trucks. Customers (including the corporations' employees) pay the extra.

Not long ago, when a General Motors plant in Ontario advertised for workers, there was widespread astonishment that so many thousands should have responded, many from distant parts of the country, and in person.

The reason was plain enough - the prospect of higher pay, or simply of a job - but it emphasized the difference between smaller enterprises which find it hard to get and keep reliable workers and which are plagued by the state's intrusions, and the corporate-union-state combination that exercises a form of monopoly.

The disruptive violence of the strike, as well as the union movement's alliance with its political arm (the official socialists) came into prominence in 1995 and 1996 in Ontario. The former NDP government had enacted changes to the province's Labour Relations Act which included a ban on all replacement workers during a legal strike together with a number of new rights:

- the right to picket in shopping malls;
- first contract arbitration in case of bad faith bargaining;
- the right to organize certain categories of farm workers;
- restricting the right of employers to oppose certification applications;
- strengthening the successor rights of unions when there was a transfer of ownership - the new owners must keep the union.

The incoming Progressive Conservative government enacted revisions which ended the ban on replacement workers, removed successor rights, and required a mandatory vote in all union certifications (formerly, certification was automatic whenever 55 percent of employees could be persuaded to sign cards requesting union representation).

This blow at monopoly - and step toward recovering some of Mr. Justice Rand's original proposals - was vigorously opposed by union leaders.

The president of the Canadian Auto Workers declared that "We are not going to accept this major setback to working people without a fight"[6] and further said that his union was "very supportive of a province-wide shutdown."[7]

The president of the 650,000-strong Ontario Federation of Labour said "This is nothing more than empowering employers to harass and intimidate and discourage and eventually defeat workers who want to join a union."[8]

The president of the Ontario Public Service Employees Union said the change "Opens up the door for them to move the services that my members deliver out into the for-profit sector."[9]

The upshot of this concerted union-leader assault upon policies that had been announced to the electorate in the years leading to a 1995 general election - and had attracted a majority of voters - was a decision to call one-day illegal strikes in three cities of the province.

The strikes were reinforced by campaigns against larger

companies, many of which closed doors for the day to avoid anticipated violence, as well as against smaller companies and retailers who were threatened with boycotts if they failed to complete union-drafted "questionnaires" aimed at the new government.

A climax was reached in March 1996 when union members surrounded the legislative building in Toronto on the first day of the Spring Session and used physical force to prevent elected representatives, as well as civil servants who chose to work, from entering the building.

This followed actions of the previous week when union pickets had blocked entry to the east door of the building to all except members of the official socialists, the New Democratic Party.

Young women were forced to squeeze between burly male pickets; one reported to work in tears, the strap ripped off her purse. Metro Toronto police refused to break the illegal picket line.[10]

A photograph on the front page of the March 27 *Globe and Mail* captured the essence of what is euphemistically called "peaceful picketing." In the foreground were three people, two men and a woman. The woman, hands pressed over her ears, was the target of the men's evident anger as she made her way past them to work. One, leaning, mouth wide, over the woman, was shouting at her. The other, hand beside his open mouth to carry the shout, was doing the same.

One elected representative, a woman, reported on television that she had tried for two and a half hours to enter the building before she found an entrance where police were able to help her pass through the pickets; pickets, she added, whose "peaceful" stance was reinforced by elbows, and knees to the groin.

That particular example, of illegal use of force to prevent access to Parliament by the people's elected representatives, led to a public inquiry by retired Supreme Court Justice Willard Estey, but it was the culmination of years of union-orchestrated violence across the land.

In his report, Mr. Justice Estey called the events "a synthesized rerun of the election" and asked: "Why is it necessary to disregard that vast network of laws and ideas and rights of freedom and expression, abandon all that and go to a coercive method of communication?"[11]

In all this, government has failed to use its monopoly of power to discharge four of its prime duties; namely, to safeguard the public purse, to secure peace and order, to enforce the law, and to exercise its monopoly of power while prohibiting private monopolies.

By exchanging its government role of referee for the state's role as player it has weakened the role of competition in the workplace, strengthened unions' power at the expense of the general public, and by these means reduced the country's productivity in an increasingly competitive world.

Democratic capitalism is not, nor does it claim to be, a perfect system. It shares imperfections with the men and women from whose individual talents and activities its strength is drawn. Nor does it claim, or even propose, to change mankind. It has nothing to say about mankind, only about mundane affairs such as the sanctity of contracts, and keeping one's word, about everyone's right to the ownership of property, and a legal system under which everyone is equal when its courts adjudicate issues of right and wrong, good and evil.

Labour unions, in the powerful form they have reached with the aid of the state and its courts - police forces also are unionized - are both a threat to peace and order and a denial of competition. Collectivist by nature, they fit naturally into the collectivist confines of Charter Law to the extent that the Supreme Court of Canada has become their champion.

When Haileybury School of Mines teacher Merv Lavigne, who was not a member of the Ontario Public Service Employees Union but was forced to pay dues to it, objected to his being fined for working (without pay) during a strike as well as seeing part of his dues paid out for causes he didn't agree with, he filed a Notice of Application in the Supreme Court of Ontario.

This was reported in the press and Colin M. Brown, founder of The National Citizens' Coalition, promised him financial support.

Although Mr. Justice White of the Ontario Supreme Court ruled in Lavigne's favour, his ruling was later overturned by three judges of the Ontario Court of Appeal.

Later still, the Supreme Court of Canada rejected Lavigne's appeal and ruled that for unions to use part of forced union dues for partisan causes was constitutional; nor did forcing people to pay union dues constitute a form of association.

Madam Justice Bertha Wilson, who wrote the ruling, made an award on costs that was not only punitive and vindictive but unprecedented in the history of Charter cases heard by the Court.

As background to these rulings we notice that Lavigne's original Application, which is a relatively simple and inexpensive procedure involving no witnesses and where lawyers argue from written briefs and transcripts, would have deprived the unions of their great advantage over Lavigne and the NCC: the unions' pockets, courtesy of forced union dues, were bottomless. (Union dues are tax-deductible for those who pay them. Unions are not taxed on the resulting income, nor are they required to publish financial statements.)

Therefore the Canadian Labour Congress and its affiliated unions applied to the court to be admitted as intervenors and to have the application converted to an action, or full trial.

Madam Justice Wilson ruled that Lavigne must pay the costs not only of the respondent union, OPSEU, but of the three intervenors: the Canadian Labour Congress, the National Union of Provincial Government Employees, and the Ontario Federation of Labour.[12]

As NCC President David Somerville wrote in *The Globe and Mail*, July 12, 1991:

> Those thinkers and writers who express concern over "libel chill" may spare some for "Charter chill." This award of costs means that any citizen seeking to defend his rights and freedoms in court through the Charter risks almost unlimited liability on court costs, depending on how many powerful groups intervene against him.

The original estimate of costs was $1 million. The final settlement two years later was $350,000, all of it contributed voluntarily from after-tax income by NCC supporters.

As a footnote to that decision, another member of the Supreme Court, Mr. Justice Gérard La Forest, was so taken with the unions' cause that, although he agreed with Madam Justice Wilson's ruling, he saw that she reached "her conclusion by a different route" and he "therefore felt constrained to write" one of his own.

In the ensuing 49 pages he held that forced payment of dues provided the union "with the stable financial base needed to underwrite political, economic and social activism."

That base would be "seriously undermined" if union members were allowed to opt out of paying part of the dues to causes they didn't agree with.

"Rather an obvious example" was the NDP and the part it had played in setting up medicare, pensions, UIC and company-paid benefits; if union members could opt out from supporting the NDP, that party's financial base would also be undermined.

Not mentioned was the fact that because at most 30 percent of union members vote for the NDP, the other 70 percent are forced to give financial support to a political party they wouldn't vote for. Nevertheless the learned judge held that opting out would reduce unions' "ability to favourably affect the political, social and economic environment in which collective bargaining and dispute resolution take place."

Opting out might even be an incentive not to join a union and would "undermine the spirit of solidarity which is so important to the emotional and symbolic underpinnings of unionism."[13]

This again is a cause of dissent. The trinity of interests - corporations, unions, and the state - is reinforced by the state's personification in the unelected judges who interpret and rule upon the codified entitlements of the Charter.[14]

The Lavigne precedent served to deny justice five years later to British Columbia teacher Norma Janzen, a 24-year veteran of teaching children with special needs, who was fired by her local school board because she refused to join a teachers union when the BC government passed a law requiring her to do so - and contrary to the Rand provision that becoming a union member was not obligatory, only dues payment.

This would have forced her to cross picket lines in the event of a strike. She challenged the law, was supported by the NCC, and like Lavigne was faced with intervention by the Canadian Labour Congress and the resulting liability to prohibitive costs. Janzen tried to get a court ruling in advance of her challenge that she would not be liable for intervenors' costs, but three levels of court turned her down.

She then asked her counsel to appeal to the BC Rules Committee to change the rules so that such applications would not be liable for intervenors' costs. Both the committee and BC's Attorney General refused her request.

Her counsel, Donald Jordan, QC, said: "So for a woman like Janzen, the Charter is a hoax. It means that she could face a bill of $200,000 in CLC legal costs before she says one word in court."[15]

On April 12, 1996, Norma Janzen, unable to face such liability, instructed her counsel to withdraw from the case.

The March-April 1997 issue of the Canadian Union of Postal Workers Union journal *Perspective* reported an arbitrator's ruling against Philip William Safire, a mail service courier in Halifax, who refused to sign a union card because he found the union's policies and constitution offensive. He stated, under oath, that he could not in good conscience join an organization he disagreed with.

The union's complaint was that Canada Post continued to employ Safire in June 1994. Safire testified that several shop stewards approached him to sign a card, but that he refused because he found the union's policies and constitution offensive. He was willing to become a member of the union for collective bargaining purposes only, but forcing him to sign a membership card would violate his rights under the Charter.

Regional Grievance Officer Jeff Woods said that the union security clause in the contract - which required new hires to join the union - didn't just deal with oaths, cards and initiation fees. "It gives the union steward the opportunity to meet each employee and explain how the union works."

Arbitrator Innis Christie ruled that Canada Post must notify Safire that he would lose his job unless he became a member of the union.

Also in 1997, a province-wide illegal strike, called by union leaders without a strike vote, put 126,000 Ontario teachers in defiance of the law.

Called by union leaders a "political protest," it opposed legislation aimed at reducing the power of teachers' unions over school boards. In contract negotiations, school boards had been no match for unions' ability to draw from their bottomless purses to fund grievance procedures and arbitration cases. As a result the education portion of property taxes had been boosted 120 percent in the years 1985-1995 during which enrolment had risen only 16 percent and inflation 40 percent.

During the strike, union leaders dominated print and electronic news outlets, asserting that the strike was a fight for democracy. Instead, it drew attention to breaches of democratic principles that union members were coerced into supporting.

It was done in contempt of the law by men and women in positions of authority over other men and women who were responsible for teaching the province's youth.

It was done while purposely misleading the public about the contents of a government bill, insisting it would give the government powers that were simply not in the bill at all.

It was done by coercion: union members who disobeyed the union leaders' orders to break the law, and obeyed it by going to work, would be ostracized and otherwise punished both during the strike and long after it was over.

This last, the coercion essential to the power of unions, was evidenced in press reports: teachers jostled, insulted and threatened by picketers; anonymous telephone calls to homes at night; identification of teachers who obeyed the law followed by heightened criticism of their job performance, even by slashing of tires.

After the strike many teachers discussed it in class; at one school students were told to wear green on a particular day if they supported the teachers' strike action. Parents who supported the government's reforms were "scared to speak out" for fear their children would be picked on.[16]

In 1998 the Toronto District School Board not only issued a misleading "newsletter" but required all elementary school students to take it home. In it, the Board claimed that funding for education would decline when the fact was that some of the allocations would rise, others would be unchanged.[17]

In a letter to the *Toronto Star*, October 22, 1998, a Grade 13 student wrote that it was nearly impossible to get through a day without feeling the effects of the confrontation. Teachers brought their political views to the classroom. If a student asked a guidance counsellor for help he would get a 10-minute speech about the legislation. Teachers voted overwhelmingly to work to rule in extra-curricular programs.

The politicization of school boards, teachers, and in no small degree children, was a natural development from the trinity of interests we met at the start of this chapter.

It was also in the interest of teachers' unions, school boards and the unionized civil servants who were responsible for drafting legislation, that union influence should spread into the infrastructure of the school system.

Thus when six school boards (including North York's) were amalgamated into a new Toronto District School Board, the new Board warned non-unionized contractors who had been doing construction work for the North York Board for 20 years that unless they used unionized construction craftspeople they would not be allowed to bid on the work in the future.

The president of the Ontario General Contractors' Association, representing 175 union and non-union contractors, was quoted as saying that the changes meant that only 10 contractors in the province could now bid on school board jobs in the municipality of North York.[18]

These illustrations of government's abrogation of its duty to encourage competition by preventing other monopolies make cheerless reading. Justice in Canada has been made costly and difficult of access, *except* to the state's hangers-on in general and, in particular, to the state-mandated monopolies masquerading as voluntary associations of workers.

Chapter 4

A new look at taxes

In an address to a Liberal gathering, and in an astonishing denial of Liberal electoral strategy, Mr. Chrétien said "I am telling you that I will not try to buy votes with the Canadian people in the next election."

Some paragraphs later he came closer to the truth with "If ever the government can get hold of some money, there are still some social programs in our society that need to be cured," and reassured the audience with "And I am not the one who will want to have an across-the-board tax cut for everybody. I don't think it is the right thing to do in a society like Canada." [1]

In other words, trust us to spend again on the social programs that sounded good in the past, even though they landed us with the debt we won't talk about, because our polls tell us that people still think redistributing wealth and incomes works; or at least enough of them do to get us re-elected.

In the Canada of the late 1990s the need for economy of effort is forever at odds with the Liberal Party's susceptibility to the seven deadly sins of politics: lust for power; pride, in electoral success; envy, as in politics of; anger, at any suggestion that Liberals might be wrong; covetousness, of the spoils of office; gluttony, for more power once attained; and sloth, in thinking beyond the next election.

It is much easier to cut spending on defence forces that comprise a very small electorate than it is on the social programs that, post-Charter, are looked upon as entitlements by a majority. In the five years following the Liberal Party's return to power in 1993, when planned overall program spending was cut by 5 percent, spending on Canada's armed forces was cut by 30 percent.

That the "beneficiaries" of social programs fail to associate them, or the Liberal Party, with the effect of rising taxes on their incomes, is an illusion that Mr. Chrétien and his followers are at pains to perpetuate. It may not be good for the country, but it's good for them.

In the 15 years from 1980 to 1995, and after inflation, transfers and taxes, the average income of lowest-income workers (the bottom quintile) rose 2 percent. In the same period, average incomes of the top quintile fell 3 percent, of the upper middle 5 percent, the middle 8 percent, and the lower middle almost 9 percent. By 1996, personal taxes, that is excluding sales and property taxes, consumed 22 percent of average household expenditure, a 15 percent jump in four years. Among those who rented, although they paid 2.5 percent less rent than they had in 199?, their average household income fell by 12.4 percent in the same period.[2]

Also banned from public discourse is Lester Pearson's craven submission to union leaders' demands for pay parity with US workers, a union "victory" which destroyed the wage gap that compensated for Canada's inherently lower productivity.[3]

By 1998, when the Liberal government's cuts in transfer payments to the provinces had cut its own spending enough to proclaim a balanced budget, Mr. Chrétien and his finance minister were quick to take credit.

While attributing the economy's low inflation and low interest rates (both of these deceptive in the face of a sliding Canadian dollar) to their wise policies of the present, they drew an impenetrable veil over the mountain of debt their policies had accumulated in the past. For behind the veil lurked a monster of some $75 billion (all governments) in annual interest charges. Almost 40 cents in every dollar of taxes brought the taxpayers no return at all.

Taxpayers who had been persuaded that medicare and other programs were "free" were forced to pay interest on money that had been borrowed in their name to create and pay for the programs. Rising taxes, and the resultant declines in real income, led many parents to seek two incomes, with the consequent disruptions of family life.

Although Jean Chrétien and other Liberals tried hard to lay blame for the debt upon the Mulroney governments that preceded them, the fact is that it originated in the governments of Pierre Elliott Trudeau. In 1968 when he won both the leadership of the Liberal Party and the subsequent election, the federal budget was in balance and Canada's national debt was about $20 billion.

Sixteen years later, when he resigned rather than face the electorate, his legacy was a budget deficit of $38 billion (54 percent of that year's revenue) and a national debt of $200 billion. By 1991, although the successor Mulroney governments cut program spending from an annual average growth of 13.8 percent to 3.7 percent, an average prime rate of 10.5 percent had compounded Mr. Trudeau's debt into $400 billion. Not long ago when the Canadian Institute of Actuaries studied unfunded liabilities of our health and social programs it found a $1.2 trillion deficit, half of it due to "free" health care.

The debt monster on which Mr. Chrétien turns a blind eye is the legacy of Liberal governments in which he served, part of the time as finance minister himself.

To quote Disraeli: "There is no act of treachery or meanness of which a political party is not capable, for in politics there is no honour."

Yet even socialism's economic and fiscal follies are less harmful than is the attitude it instills in the people.

Adam Smith wrote that "there is a great deal of *ruin* in a nation," and the truth of his observation is evident to older Canadians who have lived through depression, war, relative prosperity and the subsequent stagnation followed by decline that have marked Canadians' bamboozlement into democratic socialism.

Even in these late 1990s, when the socialistic fallacies are playing themselves out in reduced incomes, falling productivity and collapse of social programs that were first sold as being "free" and then prolonged far beyond the danger point by being elevated to "a sacred trust" - even now, Canada is plainly a whole lot better place to live than almost anywhere else on the globe.

It is not so much that it could be a whole lot better than it is now as that, unless we understand the cause of our current stagnation and decline, we shall fall further and further behind our competitors in the world's economy to a point where recovering our former standards is no longer possible.

The temptation upon Canadian prime ministers to travel abroad in order to escape the awkward questions that are prompted by their failings, applies equally to ministers of finance. Hobnobbing with colleagues in Group of Seven conferences or the International Monetary Fund reassures them that the mess they left behind is not unique. Canadian finance ministers take temporary leave of absence from a tax system of such labyrinthine complexity as to defy any attempt to simplify it: the only way is to scrap it and start again.

Vis-à-vis the United States, by far our largest market and strongest competitor, Canada suffers from three natural disadvantages.

. Great distances between major urban centres, and thinly spread populations outside them, impose high costs of distribution.

. A harsh climate imposes high costs of heating and storage.

57

- A population one-ninth the size that of the US is a correspondingly smaller market for goods of all kinds; economies of scale that benefit US enterprises are denied their Canadian competitors.

These natural disadvantages oblige Canadians to practice economy of effort, to be ingenious and innovative, and to exploit to the full their domestic market.

Comes the taxman to discourage them.

Instead of encouraging people to seek new ways of doing things and to expand their activities in the rightful expectation of reward, the taxman makes it clear in advance that much of any reward will be siphoned off by the intrusive state.

The design fault rests in a misunderstanding of what taxes are for.

The dictionary defines tax as a compulsory contribution levied upon persons, property, or business for the support of government.

But in Canada, the *role* of government has been changed.

For the first century after Confederation, government's role was in the classical liberal tradition. It protected the natural rights of Canadians who were free to do anything that did not infringe upon the natural rights of their neighbours.

Since Pearson's installation of "universal" social programs, since Parliament's rules were changed in 1969 to limit debate and strengthen the governing party, and especially since 1982, when an entirely different set of rules superseding Parliament's sovereignty was embedded in the Charter - since then, government has become the leading player in a national game of beggar-my-neighbour.

Instead of taxes being devoted to protecting people's natural rights so that they can go about their business of creating wealth, taxes are diverted into funding the activities represented by 61 agencies of the *federal* government that are listed in the blue pages of the 1998-99 Toronto telephone directory. These, as well as 33 agencies of the Ontario provincial government, are creations of a tax system which has been turned into a fund-raiser for the distributive mechanisms of a paternalistic welfare state.

In that kind of state, where remote agencies and their staffs try to do good at a distance by robbing Peter to pay Paul, Peter is discouraged from making a profit because profit is regarded as an outcome of greed and selfishness.

During a 1996 civil service strike, when OPSEU's president charged that the Harris government's proposed changes to Ontario's labour law would "open up the door for them to move the services that my members deliver out into the for-profit sector," she parroted the socialist line: profit bad; non-profit good. Thirty years of socialistic experiments in Canada have proved that the opposite is nearer the truth.

Profit is what's left over after all expenses have been met. It is the sweat equity that accumulates over years from an entrepreneur's long hours of work. It is what the housewife saves by practicing economy, what the young men and women save from their after-school jobs to put themselves through university, what a corporation earns on behalf of its shareholders.

Profit is the driving force behind the daily struggle of business managers and proprietors to practice economy of effort and remain solvent.

Of course this is selfish, in the same way that self-preservation from all perils and dangers of the night is selfish. Insolvency of a person or a firm is a tragic event; of a nation it is a disaster.

Yet in Canada a business enterprise's profit is taxed. The enterprise is discouraged from making a profit. This encourages it to increase expenses which are deductible from profit before tax, for example by borrowing, because the cost of borrowing for investment purposes is deductible from taxable income.

It encourages businesses to make management decisions for tax reasons that would not be made otherwise, also to seek favourable tax rulings, such as provisions for accelerated depreciation that have the effect of deferring taxes and providing the enterprise with interest-free loans from the government.

In short, profit is a measure of a firm's efficiency; taxing it has the effect of impairing its efficiency.

Because the tax on profit is inefficient, and has shown itself to be inefficient through a steady decline of revenue from that source, so has the state increased its tax upon individuals to compensate.

This discourages individuals from trying to increase their earnings, because they see too much of any increase taken away in taxes that appear excessive compared to the services the taxes are supposed to pay for.

By 1998, the Department of Finance projected that a combination of interest payments, spending cuts and increased taxes would reduce the value of every dollar paid in taxes to 68 cents' worth of government services.

And that was only an average. Canadians in the donor

provinces - Alberta, British Columbia, and Ontario - would get only 50 cents' worth, while the middle class taxpayers who bear the brunt of taxation might get as little as 30 cents' worth of services for every dollar they are taxed.[4]

In short, 30 years of socialism and a paternalistic welfare state had come home to roost in Canada just the same as they had after even longer periods in Eastern Europe.

In contrast to Jean Chrétien's stubborn belief in "enforcement" by a strong central government was Czech President Vaclav Havel's voice from experience: "What we have to fear is the emergence of an authoritarian government...A great many people would like to have, at one and the same time, freedom and all the material security given to them by a paternalistic state. The two objectives are completely incompatible."[5]

Discouraging individual Canadians from increasing their earnings, and consequently their spending, stops the domestic market from growing.

This denies Canadian enterprises the economies of scale that accrue to their American competitors, prevents them from reducing costs and prices that would otherwise benefit Canadian consumers, and thereby reinforces the tax effect: the domestic market stagnates, Canadian goods and services are made less competitive, and unemployment rises.

High levels of unemployment in Canada - roughly double the rate in the US - add to the costs of Unemployment Insurance and other social programs. This keeps taxation levels high, and further discourages consumer spending.

Flat, or reduced, consumer spending is reflected in reduced earnings by businesses and therefore in reduced tax revenues to governments. Whether governments raise taxes or borrow in consequence the effect is the same - to raise the cost of government without a compensating benefit to the community.

A side effect of tax growth, and of an apparent misfit between tax-paid and tax-benefit, is the growth of Canada's underground economy, estimated at $40 billion by 1985. But instead of attacking the root cause, Ottawa hired more tax collectors - 600 between 1993 and 1996, with 800 more planned by 1999.[6]

Underground economies grow from a widespread feeling that taxes are too high, that much of the money taken is wasted, and that if people are to fulfill their natural desire to improve their own prospects it will have to be at the government's expense.

All this leads to a distrust of and aversion toward government which is really directed at the intrusive state, and which could be expected to dissipate if government were to quit the field of play and resume its role of referee.

Just as socialism *always* leads to coercion, so is it time for Canadians to consider a different proposition: that freedom works.

Those two Canadian attributes - of politeness, and refraining from interfering unless help is sought - are precisely the right ingredients for a free market economy.

"Free market," as John Ferguson points out, relates not to the market itself but to participants in the market. They must be free to act in their own interests, provided they do not restrict or in any way infringe upon the freedom of others to do the same - the classical liberal view.

Underlying any system of taxation is the matter of property rights. Whether the property is real, that is, made up of material things such as a house or other buildings, or fungible, that is, made up of exchangeable things such as income, or investments, or intellectual accomplishment, property is intimate and personal.

Yielding part of it voluntarily to others brings its own reward. Yielding a just proportion of it to government for its just purposes, so that what remains may be protected from infringement by others, meets the criterion of self-interest.

But being forced to yield more than a just proportion to the state for purposes that are both ill-defined and unrelated to one's personal interests is repugnant.

When the Liberal Party got itself elected in 1993 by promising to create jobs and to scrap the Goods and Services Tax ("We hate it and we will kill it," Prime Minister Chrétien told the Commons on May 2, 1994), it was both wrong and right in those two intentions.

Government cannot create jobs. Its job is to provide a climate in which people do so by pursuing their own best interests in a free market.

As we shall see, foolish government policies destroy jobs and prevent their creation. Providing a climate of freedom is fundamentally at odds with the strong central government to which the natural governing party is dedicated.

But scrapping the GST, provided it were done as part of genuine tax reform, would be beneficial to everyone.

It was introduced by a previous (Progressive Conservative) government to replace the Federal Sales Tax, dating from 1924, which was applied to a narrow base of mostly manufactured items, generally at a rate of 13.5 percent.

The FST, it was claimed, was drawn from too small a tax base, was being avoided by many businesses, and it discriminated against Canadian producers in favour of importers (the former had to pay it, the latter didn't).

Instead of being hidden like the FST, the new Goods and Services Tax of 7 percent was touted as being "visible" as if that were a virtue. Applied across the board through all stages of production and distribution, what it did contribute was a fresh set of passages in the labyrinth.

Because the GST is a tax on personal consumption, the end consumer pays the tax. But to avoid taxing on tax, entities in the production chain that are obliged to pay the tax can apply to recover some of it through a special tax credit.

The costs of production are subject to an additional 7 percent on the goods and services purchased or performed at every stage from source through manufacture to the point of sale. There, the retailer acts as tax collector (twice: once for provincial sales tax, again for GST). The miner or farmer, the transporter, the manufacturer, the distributor, do their paperwork to get refunds, the end purchaser pays 7 percent, and, in theory, the government which didn't get enough from the FST gets more, and from a broader base at a lower rate, through the GST.

But not in practice. In its last year, the FST delivered $17.7 billion of revenue; in 1995-96, the GST delivered $16.4 billion. But in that year of 1995-96 the gross amount *collected* ($37.9 billion) was $21.5 billion more than the net amount that was finally *paid* to the government ($16.4 billion) after refunds. The $21.5 billion was paid back in GST credits to businesses, municipalities and hospitals, and low income earners, as well as repayment for governments' internal transactions wherein departments pay GST and then claim it back again.

But the tax credits were up by $1.7 billion from 1994-95. In April 1996, therefore, the Liberal government cut or removed tax credits on second-hand items such as cars, recreational vehicles and furniture, thus recovering "lost" revenue by raising the end prices to consumers.[7]

In short, a multitude of taxpayers shuffled paper in a national scramble to get back what had been taken. More than twice too much had been collected by means of a tax that everyone, including the prime minister, hated, and that many people simply dodged if they could.

When 893 citizens responded to a *Toronto Star* telephone poll on May 17, 1993, which asked if they had ever paid cash for goods and services to avoid sales taxes, 847 of them said they had.

This is madness. Yet it exemplifies ideas that discourage entrepreneurship and the other positive qualities that contribute to the creation of wealth.

Bearing down upon them is a load of state-imposed burdens: income taxes, GST, PST, UIC, CPP, health tax, Workers' Compensation, excise taxes, duties, licence fees, capital tax, capital gains tax, surtax, property tax and business tax.

After listing them and lamenting the ever-changing rules, regulations and paperwork - "a sinkhole that swallows an entrepreneur's precious time and capital" - one Ontario businessman concluded that until government stopped killing off businesses and jobs before they became self-sustaining, the job crisis would continue. Until that happened, he wrote: "I, for one, will *never, ever* hire another employee again."[8]

Two examples illustrate the dampening effect of the GST on business and private affairs.

In the first, a fledgling business needed a specialized machine made in the US. Although the manufacturer met the entity's cash flow problem by providing a long-term lease with very little cash down, at the border Canada's taxman demanded $50,000 for GST on the whole $700,000-value of the machine.

By 1996, the company was employing about 30 people and exporting all over the world - but the GST almost stopped this from happening.

The second instance traced the GST's effect upon a young couple who had saved enough for a 5 percent down payment on a $150,000 home.

The $150,000 price included almost $10,000 in GST, of which the builder got about $3,600 rebate. The remaining $6,400 of GST in the price, at 7.5 percent interest, raised the couple's mortgage cost by about $44.75 per month, or $16,000 over the life of a 30-year mortgage, just to give the taxman $6,400.[9]

How does all this square with Canadians' need to practice economy of effort, to be ingenious and innovative, and to exploit to the full their domestic market? Clearly it doesn't.

An army of politicians, civil servants, consultants, tax

accountants, lawyers and lobby groups has concocted a system that is nothing less than a tragedy of the commons.

Each contributor to the maze sees his own tiny benefit while the surrounding populace suffers in a stagnant economy that should be thriving, and in a country blessed with bountiful resources that is robbed of its potential by declining productivity.

Liberal Finance Minister Paul Martin was praised for reducing the federal government's deficit, yet he did it by raising taxes and chopping transfer payments to the provincial governments: it was their finance ministers who had to cut programs, and suffer the wrath of the voters, while the federal government, which launched us on the road to debt, drew only praise.

None of this showed any change of Liberal heart. In 1995 Mr. Martin assured a Liberal gathering that deficit reduction "must proceed apace, but the payoff will come in the form of renewed government activism down the road."[10]

In other words, a temporary return to the federal ideal of divided powers would bring two advantages: first a lower federal deficit would restore international confidence; and second, laying the blame on provincial governments for the cuts would persuade voters of the need for the "strong central government" that the Liberals wanted all along.

Not even Liberal sleight of hand can hide the fact that deficits are only the visible markers of the Canadian economy's underlying weakness. Boasting that the federal deficit in the 1996-97 fiscal year might be "only" $18 billion diverted attention from the fact that four annual deficits had added about $100 billion to the national debt since the Liberals were elected.

In 1997, Ottawa paid $45 billion - 32 percent of revenue - for interest on the federal debt; add the interest on provincial debt, and about 40 cents of every tax dollar went to interest. In short, about two-fifths of the taxes Canadians were forced to pay brought them nothing in return.

Whereas other federations manage with a relative handful of responsibilities at the national level, Switzerland with seven and the US with 15 (the UK also has 15), Ottawa has 28 full cabinet ministers, while as I mentioned before there are 61 federal agencies listed in the 1998-99 Toronto telephone directory.

When he attended the Francophonie summit in Benin, Quebec Finance Minister Bernard Landry was "accompanied by three or four people while Ottawa sent 50 people."[11]

Although this suggests that lopping off a few billion dollars from the federal budgets should be a simple matter, we have to be practical. It's not going to happen, at least not under the Liberals. What could happen, if enough voters were persuaded that it not only made sense but was also practical, is a root and branch reform of the present ridiculous tax system.

The source of the nation's wealth is the creative efforts of individual Canadians; government's duty is to secure to them the results of those efforts after taking a just proportion for its own activity.

The socialist idea that government can manage the economy and equalize outcomes is the prime contributor to Canada's tax madness.

The country's 964,789 enterprises provide employment in 522 occupational groups that comprise 27,000 separate job titles (1997).

Primary industries, communications, factories, wholesalers, retailers, restaurateurs and the whole host of small and medium enterprises that employ a majority of Canadians - running every one of those components of the Canadian economy from day to day stretches the abilities of their owners and managers to the limit, and they are frustrated at every turn by politicians and public servants who think they can set rules to manage the whole thing.

The tax madness is rooted in envy. He earns more than I do; therefore, he should pay more tax than I do, not just more in sum but more in proportion. His investment has appreciated in value; therefore, he should be taxed on the increase.

Those two injustices alone create harmful distortions.

The additives of "progressive" income tax tend to be paid by employers who wish to compensate deserving employees for the tax increase by paying them more than they would otherwise. This drives up the entity's costs, drives up prices in response, and impairs productivity.

Taxing capital gains discourages investors from realizing them, and thus reduces the mobility of capital. On the individual there is a perverse effect: by the time the gain is realized - often at death - its worth will have been eroded by inflation to little more, even less, than the original cost, yet the tax is calculated on the face amount of the gain.

In short, government-as-state assumes an impossible task: to manage an economy that depends upon the concerted and individual efforts of millions of Canadians every one of whom is different from all the rest.

Government's inevitable failure to achieve the impossible leads it into trying to alleviate some of the consequences.

Because its intrusions cause the economy to stagnate, because a stagnating economy is also uncompetitive, and less productive than it could be, fewer people are employed in it. Therefore the government devotes tax revenues to unemployment and other social programs to support people who are prevented from supporting themselves and their families.

The ensuing increase in expenditure is further increased by the political effect: political parties promise more material benefits in order to get elected.

Often the cost of the promised benefits outruns revenue, and governments borrow. Government debt grows. To pay the cost of borrowing, and to pay the cost of increased material benefits, governments seek more revenues. Taxes rise and the cycle continues until insolvency threatens and governments are forced to economize.

Then, the most vulnerable, they who are on the lowest rungs of the income ladder, or on welfare, suffer deprivation. Many of them have been lured into dependence upon the state's subsidies and have lost the will to work, the will to assume responsibility for their own welfare.

Why is it, a reader might ask, that a corporation is taxed on the relatively small part of its income that survives as profit, while I, as an individual, am taxed not only upon any profit (savings) and any capital gain I am able to make, but on my income as well?

Why is a corporation allowed to deduct the expense of borrowing for productive purposes while I am not allowed to deduct the cost of borrowing to buy and maintain the house I must live in to be productive?

Why can it deduct expenses it incurs to earn income while I cannot?

Why can it deduct the depreciating value of assets such as plant and machinery that contribute to its productive capacity, while I get no allowance for the depreciating value of assets such as a car and clothing and household equipment that contribute to mine?

These are fair questions, and I suggest the answer is twofold.

First, corporations are one of the trinity of interests - corporations, union leaders, and politicians - which runs counter to the interests of the people.

Politicians know that every union member has a vote. Corporations are valued for their financial support. This is not part of a "corporate agenda" any more than what union leaders do is part of a "union agenda" or than what politicians do is part of a "political agenda."

All three participants are doing what comes naturally and looking after their own best interests as well as they can: corporations to remain solvent; union leaders and politicians to keep their jobs.

Second, corporations, and their successes or failures, represent very visible evidence of the Canadian economy's performance on the world's stage.

That performance, publicized daily through financial media, touches many aspects of government policy: fiscal; immigration; employment; training; social programs. It also reflects to the world Canada's standing in the comparative tables and indices assembled by agencies of the United Nations and other international bodies which Canadian prime ministers delight in flaunting before domestic audiences.

Above all, even moderately successful performance contributes to the natural governing party's abiding obsession: to get re-elected.

A review of the tax madness suggests that if complexity and unfairness have failed, as they obviously have, then simplicity and fairness are likely to succeed. This leads us to look for a common element among the components of the national economy. What makes it tick? What is it that corporations and smaller enterprises, and investors, and Canadians as individuals and taxpayers - what is it that they all share?

I suggest that the common element is income.

Individual income has come to be regarded as a prime target for the taxman, yet his aim has been deflected to it by the trinity of interests and the tax system's own failings.

This brings us back to the fundamental importance of property rights and to the realization that, for perhaps a majority of Canadians, *income* is their most precious property.

It reminds us of a complaint against the Federal Sales Tax: that it was drawn from too small a tax base, was being avoided by many businesses, and that it discriminated against Canadian producers in favour of importers.

Then again, we asked why the tax deductions, that have been made available to corporations in their pursuit of income, were not made available to us in pursuit of ours?

These considerations lead us to the possibility that taxing the common element of all the Canadian economy's constituent parts on a common basis might do the trick.

The possibility is strengthened when we recall government's duty to govern by the rule of law, to enforce the law, and by these means to protect us and our property from infringement by foreigners (through defence by Canada's armed forces - which today has been eroded by government's insolvency), by other Canadians (through police and courts), and by government itself (except through expropriation after due process).

That service of protection is invaluable. It affects our lives, our property, and our continuing ability to earn a livelihood.

From this it follows that government's duty of protection, and the citizens' duty to pay for it, meet at the point of property.

Government protects our property. Its protection enables us to earn the income which for most of us is the chief part of our property. Therefore, the tax that pays for the protection should be levied on the income that the protection enables us to earn.

Here we meet a contradiction. Most of an economy's goods and services are produced by business enterprises. In order to survive, every business enterprise must earn enough income to meet expenses and have enough left over, after providing for research and renewal, to pay some income to its owners.

We can understand the need for the proprietor of a convenience store, after he has paid his suppliers for goods, his landlord for rent, his insurer and so on, to pay himself so that he can feed and house his family.

We, or at least we as represented by our governments and their taxmen, fail to relate that simple example to stores or other entities that have grown into corporations.

When one of them does so, and jumps from private ownership by an individual to "public" ownership by many individuals, it offers those individuals a share in the ownership; they become shareholders.

After that, two things happen.

First, the entity produces goods or services, sells them at competitive prices so that it can pay its suppliers for materials, and so that it can pay its shareholders the income *they* have earned by investing some of their income in the entity. That's the first thing.

The second thing that happens is that the entity must not only pay its shareholders, it must continue to pay them, and in such a manner as to make its shares attractive in the marketplace against future needs; securing a profit is a cost of continuing business.

In short, the "profit" that is owed to the entity's owners, the shareholders, is the same as what the convenience store owner pays himself. But the amount is small when compared to the *income* the store and the corporation must earn to meet expenses and pay suppliers.

This, then, is the contradiction. A business entity's profit, which is small compared to income, and sometimes non-existent, is taxable, but its income is not taxed in the same way as an individual's income is taxed. Yet for both the business entity and the individual, income is needed for survival, and government's protection must be paid for.

Profit is a cost, the cost of attracting equity capital. It is also part of an entity's total costs: cost of purchases, cost of adding value to them, cost of sales, cost of profit, cost of taxes. This goes on all the time. Income is earned from sales, payments are made to suppliers, wages and salaries are paid.

In each accounting period, enough remains from earned income to recover most of the total costs of production incurred in the previous period and to pay for costs as they come in.

An entity's earned income, therefore, consists of what it earns from production and sales, plus any part of profit withheld from shareholders for reinvestment in the operation, plus any money borrowed.

All this keeps the business going. Before the entity existed, none of the activity would have taken place, no value would have been added to the purchased materials, none of the products would have been sold and there would have been no profit. The entity created new wealth.

Experience shows that if you tax something, you get less of it. Taxing the profits of corporations has driven them to seek ways to reduce the effect, and the result has been to shift tax burdens to individuals. But a worse effect is seen in what happens to productivity.

In the 1990s federal and provincial taxes took about 35 percent of profits, but as a share of all governments' revenues, profits taxes fell from about 19 percent in the 1950s to 5.4 percent in the 1990s.

By contrast, in the two years 1989-91 alone, revenue from personal income taxes rose 26 percent, while in 1992 tax revenue from personal incomes was almost ten times as great as it had been in 1950.[12]

But hidden within the corporations whose profits were taxable was a thrust toward adding to costs for the sole purpose of being able to deduct those costs from profits and so reduce tax.

Since the measure of every business entity's efficiency is its ability to control costs, that is, to practice economy of effort, by inducing it to do the opposite and add to costs, the profits tax is a drag on productivity.

By one simple change of definition; that is, by recognizing that a corporation's profits are part of its costs of producing goods and services, and by applying a low rate of tax to all of its income from productive activities, the taxman could achieve far more than he hoped, and failed, to achieve by replacing the FST with the GST.

Instead of merely collecting the same amount as before, which he failed to do, and imposing on society the mad maze of over-collection and refunds, which he succeeded in doing, he could raze the maze and reverse the drag on productivity. Because the amount that a corporation spends to produce goods and services is roughly equal to its earned income, it would have the strongest incentive - taxation - to reduce costs in order to reduce tax.

Taxation would work in harmony with business instincts instead of against them.

It remains to apply the same method to the two other components of Canada's revenue sources: personal income from wages and salaries; and investment income (chiefly interest, dividends, and rental income).

The three together, businesses, wage/salary earners, and investors - that is, the producers and consumers of wealth - constitute the taxable portion of Canada's Gross Domestic Product. (The published GDP is understated because it excludes income earned in the underground economy, as well as income earned by co-operatives, credit unions, and certain government utilities.)

Let us look at some figures from the 1992 National Accounts that might result from applying a flat rate of 15 percent to those three sources of income, *after* deducting $6,456 from the wage/salary total for each member of the employed labour force (12,333,000 in 1992) to protect the needy.

John Ferguson estimates that 15 percent applied in that manner to those sources would have delivered $164.157 billion to the federal government in a year when its budgetary expenditure was $156.675 billion (including $38.292 billion interest on the public debt).

Instead of a deficit of $34.643 billion, there would have been a budgetary surplus of $7.482 billion toward debt repayment. At a flat rate of 16 percent, the surplus would have been $18.426 billion; at 17 percent, $29.37 billion.[13]

I should emphasize that the ensuing surplus would have been achieved *solely* from the single source of flat tax on the three kinds of income. None of the built-in disincentives to productivity described by Howard Levitt in chapter 3, and all of which are taxes in disguise, would be there anymore because the purposes they serve would be encompassed within the government's revenue from the single source of the flat tax on incomes.

The fact that these conditions of surplus are within reach, from the single source of income, re-emphasizes the absurdity of the accumulated muddle that delivered Canada's annual deficits.

Let us consider some of the prospects if the change were made.

- Government would be able to meet its obligations, particularly that of Defence which has borne the brunt of budgetary retrenchment.

- Significant reductions in personal income tax, as well as the removal of GST and capital gains taxes, would increase disposable income and living standards.

- People would make decisions for social and economic reasons rather than tax reasons.

- The time spent in preparing tax returns would be cut beyond our present imagining.

- The armies of tax accountants, consultants and lawyers would be disbanded, releasing their members for productive work.

- Families that have been forced by excessive taxation to seek two incomes to meet household expenses might find that one was enough. If a spouse preferred to continue working, the increase in after-tax income would the more readily pay for domestic help.

- People would have more disposable income for children's education and for contributing to RRSPs for retirement.

- In a more prosperous economic climate they would be better able to participate in charitable activities and so supplement tax-paid social services.

- Knowing in advance their personal tax liability, and at a low rate, people would have little incentive to avoid taxes or to engage in an underground economy.

. Because business entities could no longer charge interest costs against pre-tax income, they would strive to increase productivity and profitability by looking to retained profits rather than borrowing for cash requirements. By the same token, individuals would be better able to compete with business entities for borrowed funds.

All these benefits would accrue from a simple substitution. A single rate of tax on the three kinds of income would replace most of the intrusive state's penalties that drove the Ontario businessman to despair.

At one blow, the prime disincentive to consumer spending - GST and provincial sales taxes - would disappear.

Provincial governments would continue to collect taxes to compensate for their services, and these would still be calculated as a percentage of federal tax. (The Quebec government, which collects its own income tax, would work out its own accommodation with Ottawa.)

But all would be drawn from the same broad base of the three kinds of income, and all would be at a single rate, substantially lower than the rates today.

As an aside, the federal-provincial relationship could change in a way that was presaged by events in 1996. When the natural governing party made a belated attempt to tackle its electoral undertaking to scrap the GST, it met the hard rock of past follies: accumulated debt and desperate need for revenue. It couldn't do without GST revenue, and it couldn't "sell" its idea of harmonizing the GST with provincial sales taxes because the two taxes were applied to different things; broadening the range of taxable items would increase taxes for consumers.

The party's solution was to bribe the governments of the three Atlantic provinces by offering to pay the difference if they would combine their PSTs with the GST. The cost to the federal government would be about $1 billion over four years.

Now this was merely an extension of the redistributive policies that are embedded in the Charter. But the timing was bad. It coincided with other moves by the party to cut its spending by cutting transfer payments to the provinces, in particular to the three "donor" provinces, Alberta, British Columbia, and Ontario.

The three provinces' premiers were quick to criticize a device that would take money from their taxpayers who were subject to GST, and hand it to taxpayers in three other provinces to ease the pain of "harmonizing" GST with those provinces' own sales taxes.

This revealed the extent to which "equalization payments" affected everyone. Quebec's premier, whose government had agreed to "harmonize" the two taxes before, now claimed compensation on the same basis as the Atlantic provinces. In short, the fallacies of equalization were exposed to public view.

This leads to the possibility that if a Canadian government were to gather the nerve, or be forced by public outcry, to raze the maze and tax only incomes, the resulting increase in revenues, and the general increase in prosperity, would allow it to scrap transfer payments altogether.[14]

As the federal revenue requirement declined; and as the present thrust of provincial governments toward streamlining their operations continued to reduce *their* revenue requirements, so might the combined revenue requirements of Ottawa and the provinces fall to the order of perhaps one-fifth of incomes compared to today's two-fifths.

All of the foregoing brings us to the question: can it be done?

The quality lacking in Canada's political leaders is spunk. For years the seven deadly sins which permeate the natural governing party have blinded them to the obvious.

But there is still a chance that somewhere among Members of Parliament there may be a man or woman, even a Liberal, with the guts, persistence, and ability to take on the tax muddle and lead a crusade for reform.

Chapter 5

Effect on Canada's armed forces of French Canadian indifference to defence matters

Resolving the tax mess alone, however beneficial to Canada's economy, would still leave unresolved the fundamental matters that divide the country. These are:

- first, the revolutionary, and undemocratic, change of our system of government to the model of the Quebec minority; and
- second, the relentless thrust by that minority's political leaders toward sovereignty for Quebec.

In chapter 2 I wrote that the paradox of imposing centralized authority upon a federal system of divided powers cannot be resolved within the present political structure. When two levels of government insist on paramountcy in the same field, no compromise is possible.

In our search for a peg on which to hang the key to a resolution, I suggest we are likely to find it already occupied by a helmet representing Canada's armed forces.

The photograph of Prime Minister Jean Chrétien in the former Yugoslavia with his helmet on back to front is symbolic of more than personal ineptitude and his government's neglect of Canada's military. Predecessor governments since the days of Lester Pearson have turned neglect of the military into a Canadian institution.

What the Chrétien picture symbolizes is an indifference to military matters that is inherent in French Canadian culture and consequently in the Quebec-dominated federal governments of the past thirty years.

In 1995, during the run-up to that year's Quebec referendum on separation, then federal Opposition Leader Lucien Bouchard's office issued a press release to all military bases in Quebec saying: "The day after a YES win, Quebec should immediately create a department of defence, the embryo of a major state, and offer all Quebecers in the Canadian Forces the chance to integrate into the Quebec Forces."

That force would be on a smaller scale than Canada's "especially in light of the Quebec population's marked tendency to favour a more peaceful option than the rest of Canada in defence matters."[1]

After the referendum, an officer from Quebec said that if the vote had gone the other way, although he thought a majority of Quebec soldiers were proud to serve under the Canadian flag, there were "others who are neutral and, yes, those who would like there to be an independent Quebec."[2]

A study released by the Parti Québécois government in September, 1995, suggested that Quebec could have "a 17,000-strong armed force at a cost of about $1.7 billion a year, including CF-18 fighters."[3]

Throughout those thirty years, while the United States led the Western Allies in the Cold War against Soviet International Communism, successive Canadian governments boosted spending - and their parties' electoral fortunes - on social programs at the expense of Canada's armed forces.

Spending on defence fell from about 20 percent of the total to less than 8 percent while spending on social programs doubled from about 18 to 36 percent.

As proportions of the Gross National Product, defence spending represents a decline from 2.6 percent in 1966 - even then barely ahead of Luxembourg among NATO countries - to 1.99 percent in 1986 and 1.2 percent in 1997.

By 1996, the forces were starved of equipment and deficient in manpower to a point where, if the civil power had called upon the army for aid in two different parts of Canada, it would have had to choose between them because the army couldn't have handled both at once.

Lester Pearson's promotion of the two founding races myth was consistent with his dedication to the cause of peace. Staking out for Canada the role of "helpful fixer" in international affairs came naturally to a winner of the Nobel Peace Prize.

At home, it accorded with Quebecers' inclination to "a more peaceful option in defence matters." Peacekeeping would become a Canadian specialty.

That the "more peaceful option" had led to severely strained relations during both world wars suggested that changing the forces' emphasis from fighting to policing might make enlistment more palatable to the francophone minority.

At the same time, promotion of the French language, once the Bilingualism and Biculturalism Commission had fulfilled its mandate "to ensure the bilingual and basically bicultural character of the federal administration," might be expected to encourage enlistment in Quebec.

This is not to say that French Canadian soldiers, sailors and airmen did not play their part in Canada's wars; many of them did, and valiantly, but not in anything like the proportions of the general population as did other Canadians.

A glance at the number of war veterans registered as members by the Royal Canadian Legion in the different provinces reveals that the numbers in Quebec, despite its much greater population (7,140,000), are about the same as those in New Brunswick (pop. 738,000) and Saskatchewan (pop. 990,000), while Alberta, with a population a little more than a third of Quebec's, has almost three times as many Legion members.

As of January 31, 1997, there were 19,442 Legion members in Quebec out of a national total of 448,220.[4]

As I shall suggest later, there is no reason why a nation's armed forces should not be diverted from time to time to a temporary duty as holders of the line between factions that are fighting either in one country or in separate countries.

But for such a temporary duty to be transformed, as it has been in Canada, into the primary feature of the armed forces' deployment and training is to weaken the bond between soldiers and the nation they are sworn to serve.

In Canada the weakening is compounded by the myth of two founding races.

The keynote of armed service is loyalty to country. Loyalty to two different ones is impossible; no man can serve two masters. Yet that obvious contradiction, together with the other of harbouring within *national* armed forces elements that prefer allegiance to a different *nation* - these are banned from public discussion.

Dedication to peace is a fine thing; achieving it is quite another. When the civil war was being fought in the former Yugoslavia it was enlightening to read Edward Gibbon's reference to that country's history in Roman times and again at the time he was writing *The Decline and Fall of the Roman Empire.*

Dalmatia as it was under the Romans was "a long but narrow tract between the Save and the Adriatic," one of the provinces of the Danube within the general name of Illyricum that "were esteemed the most warlike of the empire," but which under the Roman government "were frequently united."

In the latter half of the 18th century, when Gibbon was writing, the inland parts had "assumed the Sclavonian names of Croatia and Bosnia" and though Croatia obeyed an Austrian governor and Bosnia a Turkish pasha, "the whole country is still infested by tribes of barbarians whose savage independence irregularly marks the doubtful limit of the Christian and Mahometan power."[5]

To my knowledge neither Lester Pearson nor any of his successors in the game of disarming Canada has offered any evidence that what Gibbon also called the "passions and interests [which] subsist among mankind" have changed much since Roman times.

What has changed in Canada is the whole concept of leadership, a change that was inseparable from transforming the country into a paternalistic welfare state.

Once you persuade people that their neighbours owe them a living, and embed the idea in the country's supreme law, you force their attention away from their own capacities and toward what they're entitled to get from the state and its agencies.

This is not leadership, but appeasement of imagined wrongs sparked by the basest of political motives. The appeasement consists in promising the people material gains at someone else's expense. The political motive is to acquire the spoils of office and to exercise power over the people.

Inevitably, Quebec-dominated governments in Ottawa carried with them the lack of enthusiasm for defence matters that was expressed by Mr. Bouchard and is reflected in Quebec's disproportionate number of war veterans.

Spending federal money on defence buttered no parsnips in Quebec save as a means of propping up defence-related businesses in Liberal ridings. When I was at Canadair in the 1960s, and a defence contract was coming to an end, the drill was to hook out the manpower charts and send the president to Ottawa where he would display to Quebec-based ministers the projected effect on unemployment in the Montreal area, a subject I shall return to.

It is hardly surprising that the growth of the Canadian state, and its accompaniment by a change of national emphasis from duties and responsibilities to special claims and entitlements, should lead to declines in morale.

When we accept both a duty and the responsibility for carrying it out, we do so willingly. We agree that the duty arises from circumstances, it needs to be done, and we undertake the responsibility to do it. It is our responsibility as individuals to do what we've undertaken to do.

If we succeed, that's it; we did our duty. If we don't, then we failed in our responsibility; it was our fault and nobody else's.

Implicit is the quality of self-discipline which is the foundation of morale. Opposed to it is the tendency, encouraged by the equalization and other redistributive provisions of the Charter, to look to the faceless state for special treatment at other Canadians' expense, and to blame everyone but ourselves for perceived hardships or injustices.

When Canada declared war in 1939, Canadians volunteered in their thousands for a variety of reasons, but chiefly, I suggest, because they knew that Nazism was an evil regime and the only way it could be stopped was by the same force of arms it had used to threaten and conquer peaceful neighbours.

From a standing start in 1939, when its three services were tiny and starved of equipment, this country of 11 million people was fielding, only four years later, the third largest navy and the fourth largest air force on the Allied side together with an army of six divisions.

Yet this salient fact of history is rarely mentioned in our school curricula. It has been so neglected by educators that within days of the 50th anniversary of VE Day a graduate history student discovered that not one of the Grade 13 students in the law class of a good Toronto high school was familiar with World War II.

After his exploratory questions were met with blank stares he realized that to teach the law of Nuremberg would be like giving flight lessons to people who hadn't learned to ride a bicycle. Doggedly, he laboured through a chronology of the war only to be met at the end of the class with the question: "What did Canada have to do with all this?"[6]

A reader may wonder what this has to do with the topic. The Second World War is long over. But it is because a prominent part of the Allied victory belongs to Canada, because modern Canada was formed in that war of fifty years ago, above all because it shows us what this country was able to do in the face of stresses and challenges that were peculiar to the time, that we need to remember what Canadians did.

> In his book *The Life of Reason* George Santayana wrote: Progress, far from consisting in change, depends on retentiveness. When change is absolute there remains no being to improve and no direction is set for possible improvement: and when experience is not retained, as among savages, infancy is perpetual. Those who cannot remember the past are condemned to repeat it.[7]

The dictionary defines morale as state of mind, especially of persons associated in some enterprise, with reference to confidence, courage, hope, zeal, etc.

Canada's great contribution to victory in the Second World War was such an enterprise, and although the national morale that underpinned it may have suffered decline, the reasons for decline are becoming clearer. As Canadians shake themselves free from the smothering grip of the state, so will the national morale recover.

Parallel with the decline has been a thirty-year assault upon the human and material structure of Canada's armed forces, whose morale has suffered also in consequence.

"In war," said Napoleon, "morale and opinion are more than half the battle."[8] Montgomery wrote in his *Memoirs* that "the spirit of the warrior is the greatest single factor in war."[9]

Thus is it appropriate to begin a consideration of national morale with reference to the defence of Canada in general, and the condition of its armed forces in particular.

It is a truism that generals prepare to fight the last war. A profession which must still apply the elements of strategy that predate the discovery of the wheel is by nature conservative. Circumstances change, but the principles of war that have developed over the centuries are changeless.

Once the aim has been determined, they are contained within certain phrases: Administration; Concentration of Force; Cooperation; Economy of Effort; Flexibility; Morale; Offensive Action; Security; and Surprise.

The principles survive in staff colleges, where the core of instruction is the Appreciation. Review of the situation; selection and maintenance of the aim; factors affecting attainment of the aim; possible enemy courses of action; courses open to us; conclusion and recommendations.

Foremost among the principles of war, as it must be in any consideration of the defence of Canada, is Selection and Maintenance of the Aim.

This leads at once from the obvious statement - that the aim is to defend Canada - into questions. Who or what is it to be defended against? Is the defending to be done alone or with allies? Is every possibility to be admitted, including armed neutrality?

Those questions prompt others. What are the features of the Canadian nation that inspire Canadians to defend it? What are the circumstances that might require Canadians to take up arms to defend their country?

It is a platitude that the world is a dangerous place. The end of the Cold War that kept the peace between two superpowers merely diverted attention to the variety of wars that persisted throughout the period and persist today.

Although none of the wars threatens Canada's territorial integrity, Canada's defence forces continue their forty-year involvement in trying to stop them.

This activity stems both from Canada's own condition and from a broad streak of idealism in its political leaders. Canada is above all a place where people tolerate their neighbours and settle differences by peaceful means. The peaceful condition at home encourages those leaders to preach the example abroad.

But the altruism inherent in "peacekeeping" is at odds with the self-interest inherent in "national defence." To suggest that by trying to stop wars abroad Canada's armed forces reduce the need for armed forces in Canada is to press idealism beyond the bounds of human experience.

However distressing it may be to idealists, war will happen again, and if Canada's self-interest is involved, its armed forces will be involved too.

Moreover, the longer Canadian forces are employed in "peacekeeping" the more will their equipment and capabilities be tailored to the "peaceful" dimensions of that activity at the expense of their true purpose, which is to destroy the war-waging capability of an enemy of Canada.

The single purpose of "peacekeeping" directs the whole effort away from the multi-purpose capability that warfare demands, and the results are plain: commanders lack experience of and practice in the art of combat, while junior officers and NCOs are obliged to concentrate on ways to *stop* other people from fighting instead of on fighting to win battles.[10]

In 1996 Canada's Auditor General reported that between 1991 and 1995 peacekeeping costs more than quadrupled and that training had suffered.

The army's main training exercise, held every three years, was cancelled in 1995; at some levels, training had virtually ceased since 1992 with the result that about 20 percent of reserve soldiers selected for peacekeeping overseas in 1994 and 1995 failed to meet the lowest requirement of individual skills.[11]

In the five years following the Liberal Party's return to power in

1993, when planned overall program spending was to be cut by 5 percent, spending on Canada's armed forces was to be cut by 23 percent. In fact, by 1997 the defence budget had been cut by almost 30 percent.

Typical, and consistent with the party's enduring policy, was to be the consolidation of NORAD command and control operations and three other air force commands (Maritime Air Group from Halifax, Air Transport Group from Trenton, and Tactical Air Group from St. Hubert) in the Winnipeg riding of Foreign Affairs Minister Lloyd Axworthy.

Soon afterwards, army regiments were moved from their existing quarters in Calgary, Alberta, and Chilliwack, BC, to a newly named "Edmonton Garrison" in the Alberta capital.

This "consolidation" was proclaimed as a job creator that would spin off 7,000 local jobs outside the military, but the political spin-off was to reward Edmonton's burghers for electing, in 1993, Alberta's only Liberals in four of the city's ridings - in three of them by a combined margin of only 287 votes, compared to runaway victories for Reform in all the province's other 22 ridings.

Nothing was said about the consequential loss of jobs in Calgary and Chilliwack.

These conflicting considerations are an extension of the political preference for political solutions. Figuring out the armed forces' role is too difficult, so let's send them to patch things up in other countries while getting whatever political benefit we can from shifting them around at home.

But they also derive from another fact of Canada's condition. Although it has been accorded membership in the Group of Seven industrialized nations, it remains, both as an industrial economy and as a military force, a satellite of the United States of America. If any foreign power were to threaten an armed incursion upon Canadian territory, the United States would oppose it.

Given the preponderance of American military power, this might be treated, and in fact has been treated, as the excuse to cut Canadian expenditures on defence, which have fallen, within total expenditures, to proportions significantly less than those of other partners in the North Atlantic Treaty Organization.

Of NATO's 16 member nations, Iceland has no armed forces and Luxembourg has a token force. Of the remaining 14, measured against population, Canada ranks 11th in spending, and last in numbers of active armed forces.[12]

Implicit in its condition of satellite is Canada's freedom from a particular constraint, as well as the resulting expenditures, that affect countries elsewhere. That the United States will not invade Canada is part and parcel of its role in opposing any invader: the undefended US-Canada border is a luxury denied to historic adversaries in Europe, Africa and Asia.

All of these factors draw us toward certain conclusions.

Canada is a peaceful country with no territorial ambitions other than to preserve and protect its own territory. Its responsibility, and ability, to protect its territory is reinforced by the self-interest of the United States to secure continental North America from foreign invasion.

Canada's dependence upon the United States' military shield obliges it to contribute Canadian forces to those parts of the shield that are capable of protecting Canadian territory.

The aim of a Canadian defence policy is to preserve Canada's territorial integrity.

At once this confronts the claims, both of the Parti Québécois and its federal Bloc Québécois counterpart, to Quebec's entitlement, upon separation from Canada, to the provincial territory as it exists today.

In short, the threat to Canada's territorial integrity comes not from a foreign power but from a disaffected minority amounting to some 13 percent of the population that wishes to set up its own sovereign state.

If the aim of defence policy is to preserve Canada's territorial integrity, this is where it comes into play. Moreover, any discussion of the effect of Quebec's departure cannot fail to expose the causes of the armed forces' decline.

The fact that successive Canadian governments have banned the matter of territory from public discussion of the separatists' claims does not mean that it should not be discussed; rather does it draw our attention to the reasons behind the ban. They are as follows...

First, a prime minister from Quebec would automatically be disqualified from speaking for Canada in any negotiations that developed from a Yes vote in Quebec's next referendum.

Second, such disqualification would apply equally to all MPs from Quebec - Bloc Québécois, Liberal, or Progressive Conservative.

Third, reduction of the government caucus and cabinet to MPs from English Canada would deprive it of legitimacy: all were elected on a premise - and promise - of Canada's preserving its territorial integrity.

Fourth, English Canada has neither a consensus, nor the means to develop one, as to the conditions it would require of its negotiators.

Fifth, such consensus, a prerequisite for negotiation, could follow only from a general election of members from English Canada to the Canadian Parliament.

Sixth, the resulting majority that formed a government of Canada would face not only the task of negotiating the terms of Quebec's separation but also that of determining how the new Canada should be constituted.

Clearly, all the above shows what a messy business Quebec's nationalists are playing with and what makes successive prime ministers' reluctance to face the implications all the more understandable.

Just as clearly, however, the separatists are not going to disappear and so long as refusal to discuss the matter encourages them to believe that Quebec's provincial territory is inviolable, so will their vision of the new state be harder to dislodge.

What, therefore, are the facts? If the provincial territory is not inviolable - in other words, if Canada is divisible, so is Quebec - what are the historic and demographic factors affecting entitlement?

In their book *Partition*, William Shaw and Lionel Albert devote three chapters to the "Myths of Entitlement."[13]

The myths of entitlement - that is, the regions a separate Quebec would lack title to - encompass the following:

- Rupert's Land, the northern part of the province including James Bay, which has been Canadian by right of transfer from Great Britain in 1870;
- the region from the Eastern Townships along the south shore of the St. Lawrence to the Gaspé Peninsula;
- the western foothills of the Laurentians, including most of the Ottawa Valley.

In a subsequent paper, the authors dispose of separatists' assertion that all of Quebec is the homeland of French Canadians by citing demographic history.

This shows that it was the forefathers of more than 5 million Canadians now resident elsewhere in Canada who opened up and developed regions of Quebec long before the entry of French speakers. More than three-quarters of present-day Quebec saw no francophone residents before 1925.

It is true that the seigneurial regions on both banks of the St. Lawrence from Montreal to Quebec City were clearly associated with French Canada.

But the Ottawa Valley, the Gaspé Peninsula, and the Quebec North Shore were opened up from raw forest by Empire Loyalists and immigrants from Britain and Ireland "100 years before les Canadiens began to leave the seigneuries to take advantage of the opportunities this development provided."

In the same way, the cities of Montreal, Quebec, Sherbrooke, Hull, Aylmer and Three Rivers, whose industries were developed by non-francophones, attracted young Canadiens to work there.[14]

The weakness of the separatists' claims to those regions of the province is critical to any understanding of the "Quebec problem."

First, it has been ignored by so-called defenders of the Canadian State, apparently for fear of upsetting the separatists, but more likely for fear of losing votes anywhere.

Former prime minister Pierre Trudeau, who "led" the federal forces at the time of the 1980 Quebec referendum on sovereignty association, made no mention of territory. Had he done so, and shown the extent to which an independent Quebec would be shorn of much of its land, the pro-Canada result might have been stronger still. At least those who cast the votes would have been better informed.

Instead he led an army of Liberals touting the material benefits Quebecers enjoyed at the hands of Liberal governments and promised that a "No" vote would be followed immediately by renewal of the Constitution - a commitment he had been careful to avoid mentioning throughout Canada during his own campaign for election the same year.[15]

Second, the resulting shrinkage, after separation, of the present provincial boundaries into an independent state of Quebec's historical and juridical dimensions along the north shore of the St. Lawrence, draws attention to the equally legitimate claims of non-separatists in the shorn regions to their right to stay in Canada.

This again suggests an eventual rearrangement of borders that might still give the new state a quadrilateral north of the river roughly 650 miles by 250, that is, about the same area as England, Scotland, and Wales which accommodates eight times Quebec's present population.

Beyond a new Quebec's western border might be a new province, for example Pontiac, occupying the region immediately east of the

Ottawa Valley. Rupert's Land might become the North-East Territory of Canada. New Brunswick's western border might shift westward to meet Ontario's eastern limit.

Third, the fact of an independent Quebec's establishment along the north shore of the St.Lawrence would solve the widely publicized fear of splitting the Atlantic provinces from Canada.

Communication within Canada as well as to and from Canada and the United States would continue unhindered. Quebec's shipping would use the Canada-US-administered St. Lawrence Seaway on the same terms as other nations. Road traffic from Quebec would enter Canada, or pass through Canada to the US, much the same as traffic moves now between Canada and the US.

True, there would be considerable movement into and out of the regions bordering the Quebec quadrilateral. But that is consistent with the separatists' intentions anyway.

Whether independence was negotiated or declared unilaterally its subsequent implementation by whatever means would involve movements of people not unlike those which have followed the government-inspired racism that is explicit in the language laws and post-referendum statements by Messrs. Parizeau, Bouchard, Landry and others.

The experience of recent years suggests that many anglophones and allophones would leave as soon as they could, followed in short order by francophones from the new state's western border who have become accustomed to working, or using government services, in Ontario. Francophones from the shorn regions who moved into the new state of Quebec might be joined by francophones from other parts of Canada.

It is hardly credible that negotiations leading to such an outcome would be smooth. What is credible, however, is that once a settlement had been reached, the implementation of its terms would proceed within a general atmosphere of civility and tolerance that is characteristic of Canadians.

The main elements of a successful negotiation would be contained in the relative advantages to both sides. These are as follows.

Advantages to Quebec.

Quebec's nationalists would get what they have sought for decades. They would be masters in their own house:

- free to pursue socio-economic goals unhindered by another level of government;

85

- free to negotiate trade and other treaties;
- free to join their partners in La Francophonie;
- free to establish a token defence force that suited their temperament and their purse;
- free to apply their native talents and ingenuity in a corporate effort that could rival the strides of newly independent states in Europe and Asia.

Advantages to Canada.

Canadians would be:

- freed from the financial and regulatory burdens of an official bilingualism that author Scott Reid estimates has added $49 billion to the national debt and a permanent loss to Canadian consumers of $40 billion worth of consumption;[16]
- freed from the dominance of one political party, voted in by Quebec's strategic vote, that has elected Liberal governments to Canada for two-thirds of this century. Without that Quebec vote, Canada's governments would have been Conservative "pretty much without interruption for 40 years";[17]
- freed to scrap the fraudulent Charter and re-embrace their traditional inherent freedom and responsibility under the evolving common law and a sovereign Parliament.

These are substantial advantages, so substantial in fact as to suggest one more reason for our Quebec-dominated governments' refusal to discuss the issue in public.

The advantages stem from the simple requirement that the government of Canada fulfill its obligation to preserve Canada's territorial integrity, but this reminds us once again of the succession of prime ministers from Quebec and their "marked tendency to favour a more peaceful option than the rest of Canada in defence matters."

In short, preserving Canada's territorial integrity calls for a resolute approach to any threat, whether foreign or domestic, and this, they are unwilling to contemplate.

Nevertheless, the catalogue of advantages to Canada grows even more impressive when we consider the effect upon Canada's armed forces.

Chapter 6

Effect of Quebec's secession upon the armed forces

In the defence of Canada, the presence within its borders of an independent state of Quebec, equipped only with a token force for its own defence, would impose upon Canada the duty to protect the new state's territory as well.

Against this apparent cost would be set the substantial benefit of freedom from two demoralizing influences.

First of these is the bilingualism policy that puts language and heritage ahead of professional competence.

Second is the presence within the forces of men and women whose loyalty is at best divided, at worst directed toward an independent state of Quebec.

The effect upon morale of substituting language and heritage for merit as the criterion for promotion in Canada's armed forces was predictable and depressing.

Active and retired service people share recollections of the semi-annual occasions that marked publication of promotion lists in their respective services. Among the scanners of those lists there was not a man or a woman who did not mutter "Not *him*", or "not *her*" as one or another of the names passed into their consciousness.

Yet, despite the lapses that accompany all human endeavours, the system worked. Most of the time the good people got promoted because their commanding officers along the way had done their jobs conscientiously, had resisted the "halo" effect that tended to favour subordinates they knew well, and had given honest assessments for the greater good of the service.

What must be the effect on commanding officers at all levels, of the knowledge that their assessments and recommendations were no longer weighed in the balance of greater good for the service, but in a different balance that was already weighted in favour of francophones?

The official abandonment of the merit principle in the federal civil service came into force on July 31, 1981, but that was merely the official stamp on a policy for which Canada's armed forces had been the guinea pigs for eleven years.

On June 23, 1970, the Trudeau cabinet had decided that the

National Defence Act would be amended so that English would no longer be the official language of the defence department.

Within eighteen months, all the recommendations of the B & B Commission's third volume were implemented, including the recommendation that, in order to staff the different positions in the French language sector of Mobile Command, "qualified personnel who can exercise their duties in French be rapidly promoted."

This proved to be the pattern for the way the merit principle was subsequently replaced by "imperative staffing" throughout the civil service.[1]

Key positions in defence headquarters were made bilingual. After a committee had made its recommendations to the general in charge of the bilingualism project, the general said "That's not enough," made all directors and their secretaries bilingual positions, and then did the same for all the directors-general.

When the Trudeau government introduced Canadian honours and awards to replace those of Great Britain in 1972, recommendations for military honours in the Order of Military Merit were passed from the selection committee of senior officers to Government House for approval in the same way that the Governor General routinely signs Acts of Parliament.

But in 1977 the list was returned with a note saying that it didn't contain enough francophones, and more were to be added, a practice that had been introduced some years before by Governor General Jules Léger.[2]

In June, 1991, Defence Minister Marcel Masse announced the planned construction of "a major new Naval Reserve facility at Pointe-à-Carcy, Quebec." It was to be "a fitting reminder of Quebec's strong naval heritage."

On March 28, 1992, Mr. Masse announced other moves. The military supply depots in Toronto, Moncton and Ottawa were to be closed and their functions relocated at a new $100 million facility to be built in Montreal.

The next month, Mr. Masse awarded, without tender, a contract for 100 utility tactical transport helicopters to Bell Helicopter Textron of Mirabel, Quebec, at a cost of $1 billion. The cabinet approved the order without asking how many aircraft were involved or the price. "All the ministers knew was that it was a billion dollars, and that it was for Quebec. Apparently, that was enough." In 1998 the Auditor-General's report disclosed (a) that the helicopters had cost $1.2 billion and (b) that the defence department's requirement had been for 40 such helicopters, not 100. Evidently, 40 was not "enough" for Quebec.[3]

Bilingualism for the armed forces was laid down in a "Master Implementation Plan for 1987-2002." At a meeting of the Standing Committee on Official Languages on December 3, 1992, Defence Minister Masse said that anglophones were the stumbling block and that what was required was a plan "that goes beyond the framework of military requirements to take on a comprehensive *cultural* connotation."

The number of bilingual anglophones in the armed forces had fallen from 5,000 in 1972 to 3,300 in 1987, and five years later it was still only 4,200 - merely keeping pace with attrition.

By 1992, among regular force officers, 90 percent of francophones were bilingual; 7 percent of anglophones.

Chief of Defence Staff General de Chastelain explained that "once officers have learned French, at the moment I don't have enough positions to put them all into an operational unit with a French atmosphere."

He also said that training of all naval reserve headquarters had been moved from Esquimalt and Halifax to Quebec City because French Canadians did not want to train in British Columbia or Nova Scotia. To encourage French Canadians to join the air force "half of our fighter aircraft will soon be in Bagotville, in a completely French setting."

On May 11, 1993, military representatives were called before the Standing Committee again. Progress was reported as follows:

. Bilingualism to be enshrined in officers' specification;
. Personnel evaluation reports would no longer be translated, requiring all members of merit progression committees to be bilingual;
. Bilingual requirement to be extended to senior NCOs;
. No officer to be promoted lieutenant-colonel unless bilingual - 100 percent of lieutenant-colonels to be bilingual by 1998;
. Cost of classifying military personnel by language $50 million annually;
. Translation costs for technical documents for patrol frigate project, $45 million; for tribal class refitting, $26.7 million; for 27 other current projects,

approximately $100 million;

- Cost of the 42 members of the Official Languages branch doing the paper work at National Defence Headquarters, $1.5 million annually.

In the House of Commons, February 25, 1994, Defence Minister David Collenette said: "We're putting on notice anglophones that want to be generals, want to be chiefs of staff, that they have to be totally and absolutely bilingual."

On March 23, 1994, also in the Commons, Mr. Collenette assured an MP from Quebec that it was possible to work in French at NDHQ. "As minister, I work in French, as do all my senior officials."[4]

The effect was noted later by Peter Worthington, who knows a thing or two about soldiering. He wrote in an article about abuses and subsequent cover-up at a hospital in Bosnia by members of the francophone Royal 22nd Regiment (the Van Doos) that "what's called the Van Doos 'Mafia' controls most senior posts in the army today."[5]

In the *Globe* of September 20, 1997, *Esprit de Corps* magazine publisher Scott Taylor reviewed James Davis's book, *The Sharp End*. Taylor wrote: "In the ranks of the army it is an open secret that there is a tremendous gap between both the standards and professionalism of our English-speaking regiments and those of the Van Doos."

Five years after Masse's announced move of the Naval Reserve HQ from Halifax to Quebec City, the new $41 million complex was inaugurated by Prime Minister Jean Chrétien, who said that it would play an important role in attracting francophones to the military. Among exhibits was "an historical reconstruction of New France troops during the period 1683-1760. The group promotes the culture and history of Quebec through public exhibitions, and is a valuable promotional tool for the Naval reserve presence in Quebec City."[6]

At first sight, setting up a naval reserve headquarters 1,000 miles from the sea might be taken as an extension of the fact that, also far from the sea, the prairie provinces are a traditional source of recruits for the senior service. But two other facts give us a different slant altogether.

First, is that all the key army support elements, as well as half the CF-18 fighter strength, are now in Quebec. Second, is that although francophones in the armed forces total roughly the same percentage as they do in the country as a whole, key posts both in Ottawa and in the field are filled by francophones.

Thus do we see, in the armed forces, a natural projection of the phoney war we spoke about earlier. Former opposition leader Lucien Bouchard's intention, after a YES win, to "create a department of defence, the embryo of a major state" in a newly sovereign Quebec, is to be forestalled by establishing *Canadian* forces there first. At all costs, Quebec must be kept in Canada to keep the phoney war going. How could changing Canada's system of government to the Quebec model be justified if Quebec departed?

It is when we consider the effect on the armed forces, not as an ingredient of the bilingualism policy, but as a vital part of the national structure, that we see the policy plain.

Using the law in attempts to force an inherently free people to do things they don't choose to do on their own breeds hostility and resentment.

In the defence context particularly, this is crystal clear. Anyone who has commanded a military unit knows that the true discipline is self-discipline. On the 25th anniversary of Canada's aerobatic team, *The Snowbirds*, a former commanding officer said, "Other aerobatic teams have fairly large egos and portray kind of a hero image. *The Snowbirds* have never tried to do that...We're not heroes, we're professionals."[7]

The soldier, sailor or airman deserves and expects not only to be given the reason for orders so that he understands them; he expects also to be trusted to carry them out. Trust between officers, NCOs and other ranks is the foundation of morale. Imposing an artificial barrier to promotion which has nothing to do with military efficiency, in fact which by hampering communication detracts from it, breeds frustration and hostility.

Emotion that stirs French Canadians is credited with fortifying the thrust for secession as if national pride were solely an attribute of the French.

Yet English Canadians are justifiably proud of Canada's achievements, and the more those achievements are dismissed in the sacred cause of appeasing French Canadians whose contributions are somewhat less than overwhelming, the more will English Canadians come to resent the source of their discomfiture.

In another example, the Canadian Airborne Regiment was formed in 1968 from parachute companies of Canada's other infantry regiments. But the next year, while the government disbanded the Black Watch, the Queen's Own Rifles of Canada, an artillery and an armoured regiment in the name of economy, it retained two francophone regiments that had been created the year before.

This reduction of the army to a nine-battalion, three-regiment infantry structure "sowed the seeds for [its] eventual linguistic balkanization."[8]

The harmful influence of imposing bilingualism on the armed forces is apparent the moment we review the effect, on the principles of war, of trying to use two languages at once.

Of the nine principles of war listed on page 79, five are directly affected: administration, co-operation, economy of effort, flexibility, and morale. Each one is hampered by trying to accommodate two languages.

Administration, which includes everything from the supply and maintenance of weapons, armament and matériel to the care, feeding, clothing and housing of personnel is done best in one language.

Co-operation between the three arms of the services is vital to the success of operations. Orders must be precise in the full meaning of that demanding word: sharply and clearly determined or defined; strictly accurate. Use of two languages defeats that purpose by introducing not only delay but also the dangers of misinterpretation and misunderstanding.

Economy of effort by definition calls for the elimination of everything that does not contribute directly to the success of operations. Use of a second language is one of these.

Flexibility demands that all elements of the forces engaged be ready to move, or to change modes (as from defence to attack), on the instant. Failure to understand, or to act upon, orders will jeopardize the operation.

Morale is the product of many things, and it is displayed in its purest form through self-discipline, when each soldier, sailor, or airman disciplines himself for the good of the unit. That, in turn, depends upon everyone being treated fairly, above all in the intensely personal matter of promotion that is integral to military life.

By abandoning the merit principle, and substituting *bilingualism* for professional competence as the criterion for promotion to the senior ranks of commissioned and non-commissioned officers, the Canadian government has eroded morale throughout the armed forces.

Almost three decades of the practice have brought demoralization to a condition of "service" among English and French Canadians alike.

A friend of mine who retired as a colonel and had commanded a fighter squadron in the late 1970s, described the way French Canadian officers were promoted out of turn:

Promotion boards review the personal files of eligible candidates and list them in recommended order for promotion. But as more and more senior officer positions were designated bilingual, they had to be filled by francophones regardless of the individuals' merit standing on the promotion list. Consequently, to fill squadron commander posts more deserving officers were by-passed. Once a post was filled, often it would be for a short term and the cycle would start again. This was a soul-destroying practice that was evident to everyone. Many English-speaking pilots lost confidence in the system and left for the airlines.

In October 1992, a vacancy arose in command of the Canadian Airborne Regiment just weeks before it went to Somalia. Colonel Jan Arp, director of personnel careers for lieutenant colonels, sent the army command a list of 25 lieutenant colonels who might serve as replacements, expecting to get a short list back which he would then re-check for eligibility. Instead, he said, he was sent a newspaper clipping announcing that Lt. Col. Carol Mathieu had been appointed.

Arp said "the brass demanded a francophone for the job because the campaign over the Charlottetown constitutional accord was in full swing." Mathieu was bilingual, had left the Airborne only a year earlier, and "he had a very strong file."[9]

In 1998, when instances of sexual harassment in the armed forces gave further evidence of the Charter's erosion of discipline, the Defence Minister's remedy was to establish an office of armed forces' ombudsman - and to appoint a francophone to the post.

In the same year, Canadians' ignorance of their military history had come to the fore following debate about the purpose of the Canadian War Museum in Ottawa. A positive outcome was the creation of a new post: staff historian to the museum. But when a man I knew indirectly from his published work - and which stamped him in my opinion as a brilliant scholar - applied for the post he was rejected in favour of a francophone. In a letter to a friend of mine he wrote that the entire interviewing process was "both formulaic and perfunctory...Not that the questions really mattered. It was clear that the board was set on hiring a francophone - hence the perfunctory nature of the exercise. As I am not one, but happen to live close by, I suppose I was invited to provide inexpensive cannon fodder for the charade of 'an open and fair competition.'"

The result of all this is that anglophone Canadians in or associated with the military suffer acute strains upon their loyalty to the point that many take early retirement, while francophones suffer the indignity of knowing that their appointments or promotions are suspect by their fellows. Worse even than those results *within* the services is the effect upon the better people, who leave, and upon good people outside the services who are discouraged from joining.

The imposition of two languages upon the armed forces, and the political use of that imposition to advance francophones above anglophones has not only eroded morale, it threatens the professional capacity of the forces to defend Canada.

That it should have been done to the armed forces a full decade before the civil service was treated the same way is a natural outcome from the record of the policy's author.

Pierre Trudeau shunned the military himself, didn't try to understand it, starved it of funds and equipment, and used it as a laboratory for the subsequent imposition of bilingualism where it mattered most to him - in the council chamber and the committee room, where forensic skill was paramount and bilingualism a weapon to intimidate opponents.

The folly of his language policy is exposed in the crucial matter of defence, where its damaging effect upon morale and efficiency is insufferable.

Thus would Quebec's departure from Canada herald a requirement that all who enlisted or were commissioned in the armed forces would swear allegiance to the Crown of Canada and swear it in English that was mandated as the sole means of communication throughout the services.

That simple necessity would set the stage for a return to the merit principle in the federal civil service of Canada as well, and to a revival of that service's former morale and reputation.

A soldier's loyalty is first to his friends in the platoon; second to his companions in the battalion; third to his regiment or corps; and fourth to his country. But in the indefinable way that patriotism is shaped, the fourth degree envelops them all.

A soldier in the Royal Newfoundland Regiment would fight as fiercely to defend the shores of British Columbia as would a soldier in the Seaforth Highlanders to defend the shores of Newfoundland.

But what of the soldier whose loyalty is to the "nation" of old stock Quebec? If he is recruited in the Royal 22nd Regiment (the

Van Doos), his loyalty may be to his friends in the platoon, to his companions in the battalion, and to the regiment in that order, but what loyalty does he owe to the Canada from which he believes himself to be distinct?

Then again, the defence of Canada is primarily in the hands of its regular force, the force that is in being when offensive or defensive action is called for. If the soldier from the "nation" enlisted because the peacetime army appealed to him, to what extent could he be relied upon to stay the course?

By chance I was serving at Camp Borden when the Second World War was declared. Among the class of provisional pilot officers under instruction was a French Canadian who resigned at once: he had not joined to fight in a war.

Aboard HMCS *Protector* at the time of the 1980 referendum when the "No" result reached the ship, an officer from Quebec burst into tears and told a shipmate that "he only joined the Canadian Forces to learn English and would always put Quebec first."[10]

Except when something goes wrong, as it did in Somalia and Bosnia; or, when re-equipment is made an election issue, as when Jean Chrétien casually promised to cancel badly needed replacement helicopters to help get himself elected, Canada's armed forces fulfill their difficult and often hazardous tasks with inadequate equipment to the best of their considerable ability and away from the public gaze.

Except at those times, Canada's print and electronic media ignore the military.

The Globe and Mail boasts a plethora of reporters dedicated to such matters as the activities of Canadian governments at all levels, business, education, foreign affairs and foreign aid, social affairs, sports, the arts, matters peculiar to Quebec and (less so) to other Canadian provinces and territories, the politics of foreign countries, but no one dedicated to the defence of Canada.

Defence is just one of those messy topics that don't seem to fit in anywhere and are assigned whenever they crop up to someone who isn't too busy at the time.

In the autumn of 1995, the Allied Air Forces Reunion's 25th Anniversary attracted 1,100 air force veterans of the Second World War from across Canada, and many from overseas, to a four-day series of events at Toronto's Royal York Hotel.

Although print and electronic media had been fully informed beforehand, apart from two squibs hidden away in the tabloid *Sun*, the occasion was ignored. No one was protesting, there were no placards, it was merely a splendidly organized celebration (all by volunteers) of an outstanding episode in Canada's history, and the media ignored it.

Symbolizing two remarkable features of that episode - the British Commonwealth Air Training Plan and Canada's magnificent industrial and military contribution to the Allied Bomber Offensive - four Harvards and a Lancaster flew over the assembled veterans as they paraded on the Sunday in remembrance of their fallen comrades. But the press ignored them.

It was inevitable, therefore, that among the torrents of articles and editorials and opinion pieces about Quebec and its importance to Canada's future, there has been scarcely a mention of the effect upon the armed forces.

Just as Pierre Trudeau thought nothing of using them as testing grounds for his divisive policies, so has the effect of the separatists' intentions upon the armed forces been left out of the discussion altogether.

If editors or politicians thought about it at all, no doubt they assumed that the services would once again sort out whatever raw deal they were handed and do what they were told in the tradition of backing up the civil power to which they were responsible.

Yet it was here, between civilian master and military servant where loyalty is paramount, that the system failed.

Part of the failure can be blamed on successive political masters' plain ignorance of the military; part, on shamefully looking to the United States for protection while criticizing its "threats" to Canadian sovereignty; part again on the media's studied avoidance of the topic.

How ironic, then, that the effect upon the armed forces should prove to be the crux of the matter. For it is there, in armed service where loyalty up and down is literally a matter of life or death, that the divided loyalty inherent in separatism is intolerable.

Here we must remind ourselves that the military is always subordinate to the civil power. In the endless debate of "the Quebec problem" the missing element is not the military itself nor even a lack of resolve by the civil power to contemplate using it, but rather a failure in the civil power to understand its role and significance.

In turn, this has arisen from divided loyalty in those who represent and execute the civil power - Quebecers confronting other Quebecers. Since it is they who are responsible for the damage done to Canada's armed forces, and they who have thereby blunted their own ultimate source of authority, it is appropriate to devote the next chapter to examining how this came about.

Chapter 7

Charter undermines traditional discipline

It is a commonplace that veterans of the Second World War have to be prodded to speak of their experiences. Relief at survival is forever intertwined with sadness at the loss of friends who were killed: "Why me; why them?" Fifty and more years after their friends died the faces are unchanged, clearer in memory than the fading photographs on the wall.

Fifty years for those law students in the Toronto high school is two of their lifetimes; for them the Second World War is further in their past than was the Boer War for the veterans who volunteered to fight the Nazis.

In the years before 1939 when the Royal Air Force was expanding and new squadrons were being formed, young officers were often commanded by or served alongside veterans of the Great War. It had come to an end fewer than twenty years before, yet we looked upon those other veterans, many of them in their late thirties or early forties, as being well over the hill, hard to talk to, and with whom we had little in common save the uniform.

How likely, then, are those 1995 law students to know about what my generation thinks of as "our war," when both they and their fathers have lived in a Canada not only at peace with the world but, at least since the end of the Korean War in 1952, at an entirely new game of keeping the peace among less fortunate nations?

In 1995, Canada's Liberal government seized the opportunity afforded it by two events to reduce even further the forces its predecessor governments had emasculated.

First of these was the accumulated federal debt that demanded cuts in spending, and where defence was an obvious, as well as (among Liberals) a politically popular, target.

Second was an incident during "peacekeeping" in Somalia two years before when a Somali teenager was murdered and a Somali infiltrator to the camp was killed. The incidents involved soldiers of the Canadian Airborne Regiment and disciplinary action was taken.

Then another incident came to light: some soldiers had made "racist" comments and others had been involved in a hazing ritual which showed recruits apparently doing what former prime minister Pierre Trudeau had invited striking postal workers to do when they accosted him on Parliament Hill ("Mangez de la merde").

But the hazing incident had been recorded on amateur videotape and when two years later it was leaked to the press it was immediately featured on TV and radio and plastered across front pages, the focus of horrified comment from coast to coast.

Either in genuine or calculated panic, and reportedly at the instance of the prime minister, the defence minister made a hero of himself by disbanding the regiment.

Since the Airborne was justifiably held in high regard by its peers in other armies as well as the Canadian public, and since the disbandment reflected on past and present members of the regiment, the effect on morale within the armed forces generally and the army in particular was profound.

Yet the apparent breakdown of discipline in the so-called "hazing" incident that was used to justify disbanding the Airborne Regiment stemmed from the Charter's application to the military.

No longer did officers and NCOs have the automatic right to enter and inspect barracks; that would now violate the individual soldiers' privacy and human rights. A warrant officer was quoted as saying he would not dare to make rounds of a barrack block without "a witness, a tape recorder and the telephone number of his lawyer."

The Charter's provisions had changed a fundamental relationship. At its root was the unquestioning loyalty one to another, product of "an unique extended family, authoritarian, caring, disciplined, close, aggressive, supportive," that was the goal of training for battle.[1]

But to the natural governing party, as to its predecessor governments all the way back to Lester Pearson, defence of the Canadian realm was at best a device to wave the Pearsonian flag of peace and brotherhood.

To political leaders, defence was a tiresome budget item in perpetual conflict with the banners of "compassion" and "caring" under which they could siphon growing proportions of people's incomes in the greater cause of getting themselves re-elected. If a Canada at war again was unthinkable, what need could there be for its soldiers, sailors and airmen to do other than busy themselves with trying to keep a semblance of peace between less fortunate nations that were actually fighting?

Yet Canada, whose remarkable record in two world wars is unsurpassed in the Western world, was itself unfortunate in its choice of prime ministers when the second of those wars was over. Pierre

Trudeau, particularly, was ill-equipped in his 16 years of office to understand, let alone to supervise, Canada's armed forces.

In a significant passage, Richard Gwyn wrote: "Time and again, Trudeau's lack of a war record has come back to haunt him, and he hates explaining why he didn't enlist. When pressed, he will say: 'I scarcely paid any attention to the news.'"[2]

In his *Memoirs*, Trudeau wrote that when he was at Harvard in the autumn of 1944; that is, after the Normandy invasion, he "came to appreciate fully the historic importance of the war that was ending. In that super-informed environment, it was impossible for me not to grasp the true dimensions of the war, despite my continued indifference towards the news media. I realized then that I had, as it were, missed one of the major events of the century in which I was living. Did I feel any regret? No. I have always regarded regret as a useless emotion. And I have never looked back at my mistakes, except to make sure I would not repeat them."[3]

Whether he regarded his aversion to military activities as a mistake is unclear. His apparent misunderstanding of the true nature of the Allies' life and death struggle against the Nazis puzzled his own generals, who thought "that either he does not understand the role of the military in a free society or just does not like them."[4]

During his 16 years in office, spending on defence declined from about 20 percent to 8 percent of the annual total with the result that when the end of the Cold War presented Canada's allies with a so-called "peace dividend," Canada's dividend had long been consumed and its shrunken forces, starved of modern equipment, were inadequate to meet the country's national and international commitments.

Civilian control of the military is an essential ingredient of a parliamentary democracy. But subordination to political masters in no way depreciates either the military as an organization or the importance of its role in the national framework.

All it asks of those masters is that they define its role and provide the means to fulfill it. That is the place where some understanding of military affairs is not only an advantage but a requirement, a reminder of Prime Minister Jean Chrétien's embarrassing photograph in the former Yugoslavia.

(Liberal strategists whose predecessors had plastered the press with the image of former Conservative leader Robert Stanfield dropping a football - after having caught it five times in succession - were at pains to keep the Chrétien picture well away from the voting public during the 1997 election campaign.)

Clausewitz's aphorism, that "war is the continuation of politics by other means," obscures a material difference between two modes of life and thought.

The dictionary defines a politician as one who is engaged in politics, especially professionally; one who engages in politics for personal or partisan aims rather than for reasons of principle; a political opportunist; one who is skilled in the science of government or politics.

The same dictionary defines a soldier as a person serving in an army; an enlisted man, as distinguished from a commissioned officer; a brave, skillful, or experienced warrior; one who serves loyally in any cause.

The politician who is assigned the defence portfolio, even though he might have served in the armed forces, is cast by definition in the mold of the Duke of Plaza Toro:

In enterprise of martial kind,
    When there was any fighting,
He led his regiment from behind -
    He found it less exciting.[5]

Given that to have reached the office of minister implies substantial experience in the ranks of a political party, he must be not only partisan but a practiced *politician*; that is to say, practiced in the art not so much of compromise, which presupposes a partial suspension of principles, as of abandoning them altogether. As Disraeli remarked to Bulwer Lytton: "Damn your principles! Stick to your party."

The soldier, on the other hand, requires to know where his duty lies so that he can perform it to the best of his ability. Whereas it suits the politician to be imprecise, lest he be charged in retrospect with neglecting a duty or failing to keep a promise, the soldier values precision above all, for his life may depend upon it.

This is not to say that determining a defence policy for Canada is a simple matter; merely that to the inherent difficulty of determining it is added the underlying conflict between two modes of thought.

The politician seeks vagueness in which he and his colleagues can escape their critics. The soldier requires precise direction so that the orders he must give in turn can be precise.

How this apparent incompatibility can be made to work in practice depends much more upon the maturity of a political master than it does upon the competence of a military servant.

Most of the time, professionalism among the military will ensure a reasonable competence at the top, but the extent to which commanders can exercise the leadership that secures competence throughout the service depends upon political support, and even more upon political understanding.

The politician's job is to determine policy, but if he is to make a decent fist of it he needs to understand both the capability and the limitations of military action. As in all matters of great import, there is a fine line between success and failure. Committing a nation's armed forces to offensive action is such a matter.

Offensive action. The phrase offends the Pearsonian image of a capital sheltering beneath the Peace Tower, home to a smiling and contented citizenry. But it is the inescapable component of going to war.

It may be comforting to think that "serious" war, war between modern industrialized states, is no longer possible. It may even be the conviction of Canada's policy makers. But history tells us it may also be a delusion.

One thing is certain: to hope for peace is no foundation for policy. Nor, in my opinion, is it a foundation for nurturing the morale of a nation. People who value their freedom should be prepared to defend it.

On the face of it, there may appear to be a contradiction between Canadians who habitually tackle their domestic conflicts peacefully, and the record of those same Canadians in this century's wars.

Then, it was not so much the professionals who acquitted themselves well, but rather the amateurs and the week-end warriors of the reserve forces who displayed qualities of leadership, of tactical skills and strategic comprehension that boosted Canada's contribution far beyond its nominal capacity.

Nevertheless, because the permanent force is responsible for training in and execution of peacetime tasks, it is important to understand the causes of the damage to its morale we spoke about earlier.

During Lester Pearson's prime ministership, the Liberals "unified" the three services into one, tossed away with their distinctive uniforms many of the traditions that bolster morale, and soon afterwards used the "unified" force as guinea pigs for imposing Pierre Trudeau's official bilingualism on the government service. Henceforward language and culture, not professional ability, would determine fitness for promotion.

Lasting damage was caused by disbanding the three service

headquarters that were responsible for military doctrine and execution, and lumping civil and military servants together in one National Defence Headquarters.

Since the bilingual program was clearly political - the central thrust was all too plainly toward accelerated promotion for francophones - and since the civilian staffs in NDHQ were long practiced in the wiles of budgetary and personnel manipulation, their military counterparts had no choice but to adopt the same techniques.

Military staff officers became at least partly politicized, those in the higher ranks more so, while the only way the service side could achieve some kind of parity with the civil side's superior conditions of service was by inflating the rank structure.

In the 1980s, after Pierre Trudeau resigned rather than face the electorate, a Progressive Conservative government restored the identity, and to some degree the morale, of the three services. Disguised as land, sea, and air headquarters of the "unified" force, the three services regained distinctive uniforms and, for a few years, some control of their affairs.

One of the first planned "economies" of the natural governing party on its return to power in 1993 was not only to close military bases but also to disband the three headquarters. While steps were taken to thin out the inflated rank structure of the service side, senior ranks on the civil side were fattened up.

This sorry tale is the outcome of the Canadian state's diversion from the necessary to the politically attractive. In the thirty years from 1956 to 1986, during which budgetary expenditure on defence and social welfare combined was virtually unchanged, the defence share declined from 35 percent to 8 percent while the share of social welfare rose from 18.2 percent to 46.6 percent.

As proportions of the Gross National Product, defence expenditures represent a decline from 2.6 percent in 1966 to 1.99 percent in 1986 and 1.2 percent in 1997.

But by 1997, as we saw before, the forces were starved of equipment and deficient in manpower to a point where, if the civil power had called upon the army for aid in two different parts of Canada, it would have had to choose between them because the army couldn't have handled both at once.

In February 1998, when the US asked Canada to join other NATO countries in a show of force against Iraq, it was acknowledged even by senior commanders that "attrition, increasing obsolescence and deep cuts in military spending had left Canada's military all but unfit for combat."[6]

Thus do we see the false economy of neglecting a vital element of national housekeeping because the fashion of the moment has made it unpopular.

The past years of neglect will oblige the Liberal government and its successors to face future years of re-equipment and renewal if the armed forces are to fulfill their peacetime functions.

The figures quoted above to illustrate the swing down for defence and up for welfare are themselves an illustration of what happened to Canada during that thirty-year period.

Whereas in 1956 Defence's 35 percent of the budget represented 5.5 percent of GNP, and had fallen ten years later to 20 percent of the budget (2.6 percent of GNP), by 1986 its much reduced 8 percent of the budget was still 2 percent of GNP.

In other words, the country's total dollar-worth grew under the influences of immigration, increased production, and not a little inflation, but much of the increase was diverted into social welfare and the expansion of governments at all levels which is inseparable from the politics of redistribution - and much of the money spent was borrowed.[7]

As an aside, we might remark again how convenient it was during those years for the Canadian political Left to bluster about perceived economic and cultural incursions by the United States; while all the time (through the Left's downplaying of the Canadian defence responsibility) depending more and more upon the goodwill of this threatening neighbour to take up the slack.

In our search for a balance between two conflicting purposes - that of the politician to keep defence spending down and that of both the military and its suppliers to keep the spending up - we are confronted with a near-total absence of opinion or even of constructive thought in Canada's media.

Since defence is one of the few legitimate concerns of the federal government in a federal state (others being maintenance of civil order, finance and sound money, foreign affairs and trade); and since the media to which we look for information excludes defence from its regular catalogue, we are obliged to look elsewhere for guidance.

South of the border, the armed forces and their supporting industry are to a scale far beyond our modest capacity, nor are we burdened with American assumptions of empire. Switzerland's geography makes its defence situation unique; Sweden's is founded in neutrality. Great Britain, from which many of our military traditions derive, is tied increasingly to Europe while retaining overseas commitments we do not share.

If this short review draws us to a conclusion that we should make up our own minds about a judicial allocation of funds to defence, we might avail ourselves of a neutral guide I have used for some years which assesses defence capabilities under a number of heads:

- spending in dollar terms;
- spending as percentages of GNP;
- percentages of population in the armed forces;
- quality of armed forces;
- rank by warmaking power.

The study was updated to 1984, a good year for our purpose because, although that was at the end of the Trudeau period of neglect, the forces still had enough residual capability to signify in the assessments.

The authors bring impressive credentials to the task and their sources range from the specialized international press all the way to Liddell Hart, George Orwell, Clausewitz, Machiavelli, and Thucydides.[8]

In each instance, the top fifteen nations are ranked according to what they spend and how they do the job, and the interesting thing is to see how the composition of the lists changes with the categories.

For example, the top three military spenders are the United States, Russia and Britain, but in the next table - percentage of GNP spent on defence - the top three are Israel, United Arab Emirates and Angola, with Russia in thirteenth place and the US and Britain (and Canada) off the list altogether.

By percentage of population armed, the top three are Yugoslavia, South Korea and Switzerland, while in overall warmaking power they are Russia, the US and China.

Canada appears in only two of the lists. In actual dollars spent on the military (then 2.2 percent of GNP), it was 14th, but in the ranking by quality of armed forces, it was comfortably in the middle at No. 8, sandwiched between Japan at No. 7 and East Germany at No. 9. Top spot in the quality stakes was awarded to West Germany, with Britain second, Israel third, France fourth, South Africa fifth and the US sixth. Russia was 13th.

The authors derive the quality assessment from "human factors such as military tradition, practical experience, and general efficiency. The most critical factor, however, is military leadership. Some nations manage to develop superior military leadership, which is demonstrated whenever they are involved in a war. In peacetime that superior leadership continues."[9]

Not a bad description of Canada's defence situation at the time.

Nevertheless, what might be called the defence establishment - civilians and military people at the Ottawa headquarters and throughout the regular force, people in defence industries; and, bringing up the rear, retired service people like me - could hardly escape the influence of the spirit of the time that infected Canada during the past thirty years just as it did other industrialized countries that are featured in the comparative studies.

When the legitimate power of government - safeguarding the citizens' property and administering the law without fear or favour - is allowed to degenerate (and expand) into political power, it ceases to become the protector of all the people and becomes the protector of particular people or groups of people at their neighbours' expense.

This brings an interloper, a third party, between people who formerly would have settled or continued to tolerate their differences in the Canadian way, and the third party bears the mighty stick of the law and its enforcement agencies. All of this makes people nervous, very careful about what they say or write, and infects them with the disease known as fireproofing.

Now that is the reverse of the spirit you want in the armed forces, but it is the inevitable result of too much government, too many regulations, too many commissions, committees and tribunals; all of them dedicated to making nuisances of themselves and thereby chipping away at our liberty.

Initiative and innovation are by-products of freedom. One of the dangers we face in Canada is that, if we allow freedom to slip away at the present rate, we shall reach a point where the qualities that freedom breeds are no longer there.

As a practical matter of finance and budget-making, even to raise the proportion allotted to defence from 1.2 percent of GNP in 1997 to 2 percent the same year would have required an increase of 60 percent, or about $6 billion, in the defence share of the 1996-97 estimates.

But that assumes a continuation of current tax and fiscal policies. The changes I suggested in chapter 4 would permit rises in the defence proportion while still leaving room in the budget for reducing the national debt - a goal which eludes the natural governing party today.

The point is that Canada's membership in NATO and NORAD imposes a duty to shoulder its share of the cost in manpower and material. Just as the years of neglect have caused serious damage to the armed forces, so will the coming years call for substantial expenditures, if the forces' capability (not only to defend Canada but to fulfill its contribution to alliances) is to be restored.

When we consider the two modes of thought, and recognize that the circumstances of politics militate against adherence to principle, it becomes even more important that the soldier, in his capacity of military adviser to political masters, adhere to the principles of war that are both historic and enduring.

To return, then, to the crucial one of those principles - offensive action - it is safe to assume that any offensive action by Canadian forces will not be undertaken alone. Rather will they fight alongside, or in support of, allied forces.

To do this implies a land/sea/air capability so that Canadian forces can fulfill the roles assigned to them in any of the military situations the allied forces confront.

It also implies a continuing requirement to participate in joint and allied peacetime exercises so that Canada's forces are kept abreast of, and practiced in, developments in offensive tactics as well as the supporting techniques and technology.

Again, this underlines the gap between Canada's External (more recently Foreign) Affairs Department, traditionally the senior branch of government, and Defence, which takes a back seat in peacetime to the extent that it ranked 14th on the list of priorities during the Trudeau years.

Supporting defence are the components of Canadian industry that kept themselves going in the barren years by seeking co-production with US contractors and trying to sell some of the products overseas. But there they ran foul of External Affairs.

For example, when Canadair had devoted years to the sale of its CL-44 four-engined transport and sought to expand the market beyond the US (where the two major freight carriers were operating the aircraft successfully) customers for the passenger version were found in Pakistan International Airlines and the national airline of Saudi Arabia, which relied on PIA for technical support.

After many months of effort, and when both airlines had agreed to buy the aircraft, External Affairs stepped in and refused an export permit for fear that selling the aircraft to Pakistan would offend India, which was busy filling its military inventory with aircraft from the Soviet Union.

Not long after that, when the Brazilian Air Force had decided to replace its aged Meteors with CF-5 tactical fighters from Canadair's production line for the Canadian Armed Forces, External Affairs pulled the same trick again, this time for fear of starting an arms race in Latin America. In due course the BAF bought Mirage supersonic fighters from the practical French far more warlike than Canada's CF-5s.

Similar problems faced de Havilland. After the company had demonstrated its Buffalo transport to the Indian Air Force, and the IAF decided it was the aircraft to fit its requirements in the varied climatic and topographical conditions of that mountainous country, Indian premier Indira Gandhi's government set off a peaceful nuclear explosion and External Affairs cancelled de Havilland's export permit.

Much has been written and filmed about the cancellation of the Avro Arrow; nothing at all about the opportunities that were thrown away afterwards by Pearson and Trudeau and their henchmen in External Affairs. Their attitude was epitomized by the comment of a senior mandarin after his department had vetoed the CF-5 sale to Brazil. He said, "Good. Now we can forget about Brazil."

The CF-5 production came about as a result of Ottawa's last minute loss of nerve to participate in a US-Canada-UK joint production of the Rolls-Royce Spey-powered F-4 Phantom, which was the RCAF's choice for a tactical fighter to fulfill both its NATO commitment and the domestic defence requirement.

The RAF wanted the same aircraft, so did the Royal Navy, and the US Marine Corps was interested if the project went ahead.

Everyone stood to gain: Canada from the export of Canadair-built airframes to offset the cost of the RCAF's order; the British from the sale of engines and electronics for the RCAF order; and the Americans from the sale of the manufacturing licence and technical support.

Unlike the Arrow situation, where there was no prospect of foreign sales, this was a tri-nation arrangement made in advance.

But after months of negotiations, in the USA, the UK and Canada, between the three governments, the military and the companies, and when everything was finally in place, Ottawa decided that the program was too expensive, and the project fell through.

Instead of Canada mounting a production line of over 300

technologically advanced aircraft, the 210 aircraft for the RAF and the RN were built in the USA, and the RCAF was fobbed off with the CF-5, already obsolescent, inferior in performance, and of which many went straight into storage.

The other project - CAMRA (for Canadian Advanced Multi-Role Aircraft) - was the brainchild of two RCAF officers, Brigadier (later Lieutenant) General Bill Carr, an outstanding all-round operational pilot; and Colonel Hal Bridges, who worked for him as Director of Aircraft Engineering.

They too had learned from the Arrow experience. As Bill described it in a letter to me many years afterwards:

"It had become apparent to us that new technology provided the performance margin which would permit making greater demands for flexibility. The state-of-the-art in 'black box' technology was advancing at such a pace as to make it reasonable to demand viable multi-role capabilities for the first time...The Americans said we could count on their releasing the technology if we were able to work up a consortium similar to that which had developed in the [Canadian-led] F-104G program. Frankly, the Europeans were delighted because this would provide the stimulus necessary for their aerospace industry to become more competitive... The whole business plan was developed by us in AFHQ as was the management plan also...both of these plans were implemented [by the European consortium] after we withdrew. They are in existence still. We withdrew because our political masters were afraid we would get locked into a costly Avro Arrow type program - even though we knew the shared production run would total 800 or more aircraft. In summary, we invented the concept, cleared the technology release, designed the production and management plans, and controlled the all-seeing all-dancing demands, and then withdrew."

That imaginative, and for the British, Germans and Italians successful project (by 1988, 706 Tornados were in service with their air forces; a Canadian order would have brought the total to more than 800), was killed in Canada by the government of Pierre Trudeau, who soon afterwards was prattling about "a third option" for Canada, by which he meant seeking trade with Europe to offset Canada's dependence upon trade with the US.

Apparently it did not occur to him that his staged withdrawal of Canadian forces from NATO might cause some resentment against Canada among the affected governments of European countries.

Defence was a blind spot with the man who, 20 years of age when the Second World War started, mocked Canada's war effort and appeared to have been ashamed, in later life, of his actions and attitudes at that critical time.

The years at Canadair taught me a lot about the relations between big business and big government, and how the softening of distinction between the upper levels of both has the harmful effect of most compromises: in the face of superior power, compromise for the lesser power means surrender. (Contrary to myths of the Left, business, however big, is always subject to the dictates of government, which sets the rules.)

Senior management was so sensitive to the whims of the mandarinate that when the incumbent of the company's Ottawa office in the mid-1960s lost favour with one particular mandarin, the company's president fired him.

It was the same mandarin who scuppered Canadair's sale of 37 CL-44 four-engined freighters to the USAF's Military Air Transport Service by advising Prime Minister Diefenbaker that it was too soon after the Avro Arrow was cancelled in Toronto for such a major sale to be permitted in Montreal. This, despite the fact that about half the CL-44 work would have been sub-contracted in the Toronto area.

As I mentioned before, when a military order was coming to an end, the drill for getting another one was to dust off the manpower charts and send the president to Ottawa, where he would display to appropriate ministers the dire effect upon Montreal and Quebec - and especially upon Liberal ridings - if Canadair were to experience the layoffs that the charts projected.

In short, purchasing decisions were made for the wrong reasons. Canada's defence forces were either lumbered with inadequate equipment, or denied it altogether, because political leaders were more concerned with their own survival than with the country's.

I learned by going there about conditions in other countries; that however badly they were run, and however unenviable the lot of the masses, there was always some money for the military.

In Latin America, bribes were a prerequisite for doing business, as they were in Africa and East of Suez. In Germany, Austria and

Italy they were called commissions, dispensed by intermediaries, and it was par for the course that the company would be expected to pick up the tab for government officials who expressed a desire to visit Canada.

In Canada, the bribery was merely political and consisted of Canadair's share of the larger blackmail that Quebec has practiced so successfully upon the rest of the country since Confederation.

Despite these built-in Canadian headwinds, the fact remains that offensive action (in which the use of air power is a key ingredient) is a prerequisite to winning battles and, eventually, a war. Let us consider two examples, one from World War II, the other from the 1991 Gulf War.

After the defeat of France in 1940 and the evacuation of British and some Allied troops from Dunkirk, Nazi Germany was master of Europe.

For three years, until the United States Army Air Force began to grow in strength, RAF Bomber Command was the sole means of carrying the war to the German heartland.

When Hitler launched operation Sea Lion, and assembled huge invasion barges in the Channel ports, Bomber Command attacked them continuously. On the night of September 13, 1940, an especially successful attack sank 80 barges in the port of Ostend alone.

Two days later, September 15, saw the climax of Fighter Command's magnificent defensive battle against the Luftwaffe, and on September 17 the German invasion plans were postponed indefinitely. Fighter Command had won the air battle that was a prerequisite to crossing the Channel; Bomber Command had destroyed a great part of the shipping and war material on which the invasion depended.

Bomber Command, the RAF's offensive arm in which Canadians and Royal Canadian Air Force squadrons played a major role, was in continuous operation from September 3, 1939, when Flying Officer A. McPherson, Commander Thompson, RN, and Corporal V. Arrowsmith first crossed the German coast in Blenheim N6215, until the night of May 2/3, 1945, when a force of 170 Mosquitoes attacked airfields near Kiel in advance of British and Canadian ground forces.

Nowhere was the effect of the bomber offensive more forcefully stated than in the post-war report by Adolf Hitler's former armaments minister Albert Speer when he wrote that the real importance of the air war was that "it opened up a second front long before the invasion of Europe," that it was "the greatest lost battle on the German side," and that "the nearly 20,000 anti-aircraft guns stationed in the homeland could almost have doubled the anti-tank defences on the Eastern front."[10]

A British historian summarized the effect of the bomber strategy in a paragraph:

"Intervention at Dunkirk, the bombing of the invasion barges, the bolstering of British morale, the mining campaign, the substantial part in defeating the U-boats and in finishing off the German fleet, the share in knocking out Italy, the help in mastering the V-weapon menace, the assistance to the Allied armies at critical moments from the Normandy landings onwards, the tying-down of vast German resources to anti-aircraft defence, the final deadly offensive against oil and communications - the list of achievements is impressive enough, whatever view is taken of the losses in production caused by area-bombing."[11]

Estimates by strategists at the time concluded that had it not been for the Allied Bomber Offensive's preparing the way for invasion, Germany might not have been defeated until mid-1947 at the cost of another million casualties among the Western Allies.

The British (and later American/Allied) bomber strategy owed much to the experience of senior airmen who had witnessed the dreadful slaughter of trench warfare in the Great War.

Whatever opinion one holds of the strategy's effect on the eventual victory in 1945, there is no doubt that it saved countless lives on the side of the Western Allies.

Military casualties of British, Commonwealth, and American forces, who used offensive air power to great advantage in every theatre where they fought, were but a fraction of those suffered by the Germans and Russians, whose use of air power was essentially land-based and tied to tactical support of the ground forces.

In the years that they were engaged, Germany and Britain from 1939 to 1945, the Russians and the Americans from 1941 to 1945, the Germans lost 3,300,000 killed, the British 271,311; the Russians 13,600,000, the Americans 292,131. Canada lost 42,042, of whom 17,101 were airmen, and of those, 9,919 were of Bomber Command.[12]

Bomber Command's great contribution to the eventual victory, in which Canada and Canadians played so valiant a part, had vanished from the scene until 1992, when a CBC "docudrama" called

The Valour and the Horror brought it briefly into the public eye.

The second episode of the series, "Death by Moonlight: Bomber Command," in which Canadian aircrews of Bomber Command were depicted as war criminals, morally inferior to the German fighter pilots who were shooting them down, was so replete with distortions and inaccuracies, and the protests from Canadian aircrew veterans and others were so widespread, that the series was placed on the agenda of the Senate's Sub-Committee on Veterans' Affairs.

Significantly, in the light of the Supreme Court's subsequent ruling about defamation and ascertaining the truth of published allegations, the Senate hearings revealed that "The National Film Board, based on a brief statement of the concept, handed over $729,000 to the filmmakers and gave them the right of final cut. They made little or no attempt to check the accuracy of the filmmakers' research."[13]

Historians and other witnesses testified to the film's inaccuracies, and the CBC's ombudsman reported that the series was "flawed as it stands and fails to measure up to CBC's demanding policies and standards."

Thousands of Canadian aircrew veterans, as well as veterans of the other services, of the merchant marine, and the general public, contributed over $350,000 toward the cost of a legal action for defamation against the CBC and its co-producers.

But the aircrews were denied an opportunity to submit evidence to the court. A motion court judge dismissed the action on the grounds that no individual was singled out and that a class of 25,000 could not be libelled.

This despite the fact that all the aircrews were members of a determinate class, identified by name in the records of the country they volunteered to serve. Worse, the motion court judge's ruling was upheld by the Ontario Court of Appeal, whose members, again without giving the aircrews an opportunity to present evidence, made up their own minds after watching the defamatory film.

Undaunted, and still supported by thousands of contributors through their newsletter, *Flarepath*, the aircrews applied to the Supreme Court of Canada for leave to appeal the two lower courts' denial of justice.

But the Supreme Court turned them down.[14]

Madam Justice Rosalie Abella, who was one of the three judges of the Ontario Court of Appeal who refused to hear the aircrews' evidence, appeared to be unaware of the near-total ignorance of

World War II even among law students.

In a minority judgement, she wrote: "Whatever we may criticize as inaccurate or misperceived or understressed in the film and its related publication, none of it challenges or undermines what we must assume most reasonably informed Canadians know to be the historical context of the film and book: that the Second World War was fought in Europe by Canada and the Allies to defeat Nazi Germany and prevent the unthinkable consequences of the spread of its power."[15]

In the final issue of *Flarepath*, the aircrews quoted Chapter 39 of the 1215 version of Magna Carta:

> No free man shall be taken or imprisoned or dispossessed, or outlawed, or banished, or in any way destroyed, nor will we go upon him, nor send upon him, except by the legal judgement of his peers or by the law of the land.

Canadian aircrew veterans of Bomber Command were dispossessed of reputation by agencies of the Crown of Canada in contravention of the common law and clearly established procedure. They were denied the chance to clear their names of defamation in the courts of the country they fought for.

In his *factum* to the Supreme Court, their counsel, Ian W. Outerbridge, QC, wrote:

> By adjudicating the question on a motion to strike the Statement of Claim, the Court of Appeal and the learned motion court judge have usurped the function of the jury with evidence and have established a rigid and unrealistic legal standard.

In a letter to me, a former judge of the Ontario Supreme Court wrote that the legal result was "probably the most startling miscarriage I have ever seen...to be denied access to the courtroom in a case brought by intelligent people - with an honest cause brought in good faith - is stunning."

Stunning indeed, yet entirely of a piece with the political attitudes described in chapter 2 that favour the collective over the individual, that encourage judges to make new law, and that put the nation's top court and its decisions beyond the reach of the ancient institution of Parliament.

The aircrews volunteered to fight the Nazi State's armed forces; fifty years later their record was denigrated by agencies of the Canadian State, and they were denied access to its courts.

The readiness of those agencies to stigmatize Canadian bomber crews as war criminals is hard to explain except as solicitude for defenders against attackers in a cause divorced from good or evil on either side. That, in turn, is an outgrowth of declines in morale, of commitment to "peacekeeping," and consequently of distaste for offensive action by Canada or its armed forces under any circumstances.

In 1990, when Saddam Hussein's invasion of Kuwait was condemned by the UN Security Council, an expeditionary force was assembled under US leadership.

In the Commons debate, January 15, 1991, then opposition leader Jean Chrétien said that Canada's duty was "to promote peace, not war," and that if there was a war "our troops should be called back, not be there if there is a war."

In the event, Canada did participate, but not with offensive action. The Canadian Navy commanded the Combat Logistics Force which safeguarded convoys and kept the front-line combatants supplied with fuel, ammunition, and spares. Canada's CF-18s were part of the air defence force protecting the massive UN air assault from attack by Iraqi aircraft.

But when the UK and the US confirmed a requirement for a 5,000-man-strong mechanized force that Canada had said would be available to NATO, the request was turned down: it couldn't be met. Instead, Canada would send a field hospital to Saudi Arabia.

Chapter 8

Demoralization of armed forces reflects declining *national* morale

Securing Canadian territory, which by definition includes aid to the civil power, is the forces' fundamental role. When called upon, they are required to reinforce the civil power's duty under the Constitution to uphold the laws "for Peace, Order, and good Government of Canada."

That duty of government to keep the peace, backed if necessary by the armed forces, underpins the successful functioning of a civil society.

Formerly this was a matter of enforcing laws that everyone understood. The evolving common law was rooted in negative rights. But since 1982, when the Charter was imposed on Canadians, laws which are obscure and ambiguous declare positive rights and entitlements that people can claim through the courts.

As we saw in chapter 7, it also changed the fundamental relationship between military commanders at all levels and those it was their duty to lead.

No longer were Canadian service people inherently free men and women, freely subjecting themselves to military discipline in the greater cause of protecting all Canadians' freedom against domestic and foreign assaults. Post-1982 they had become wards of the anonymous state, entitled to "benefits" which overrode the discipline that must infuse fighting services if they are to do their job.

The difference is plain: negative rights leave decisions about abiding by or breaking the law to the individual; positive rights put decisions in the hands of the state, its tribunals and commissions, and its unelected judges.

All these factors bear upon the armed forces. When citizens habitually obey the laws, the civil power needs no aid from the military. But when the nature of the laws is changed to cause dissent, so will the task of keeping the peace grow in complexity; so will the military's duty to reinforce it grow in importance.

At the same time, in line with the law of unintended results, the Canadian forces' long experience of peacekeeping abroad would be put to a more practical use at home during the period of adjustment that accompanied a Quebec decision to leave the federation. (It might also be needed in Canada's most populous province if the union movement there persists in its thinly-veiled revolt against civil order.)

After the period of negotiation and migration that accompanied a separation, the two countries would enjoy the corresponding advantages.

Quebec's defence force would be able to concentrate on guarding its southern border on the river. The much wider responsibility, of securing the Canadian territory, would fall, as it does now, to the Canadian Armed Forces in co-operation with the US military.

Development and review of joint defence planning between Canada and the United States is inherent in the structures of NATO and NORAD. But successive Canadian governments' neglect of the armed forces has relegated them to a role as very junior partner both in the defence planning and in the tactical exercises that put plans to the test.

A first step toward raising Canada's profile in those joint endeavours would be a commitment by the government to increasing the defence share of annual budgets until it reached a percentage of GNP that would put Canada at least in the same league as other NATO countries.

Responsibilities for border security are laid down in the statutes, but they are also self-evident. The smuggling of drugs or other contraband into Canada by whatever means, because it violates Canadian criminal law, is a matter for the police.

If the circumstances exceed the capability of police forces to deal with them, as for example when aircraft suspected of smuggling are detected on radar screens, the air force's capability to intercept and track them will complement the police operation. Similarly, if naval force were needed to arrest a merchant vessel, the armed forces would do that too.

These interventions by armed forces on the domestic scene copy duties they perform under UN or NATO authority when sanctions are applied against warring states. They are extensions of the armed forces' duty to give aid to the civil power. Customs officers have power of arrest; immigration officers can also detain on suspicion; both can call upon the police if necessary.

It goes without saying that, in a country at peace, especially in one as inherently peaceful as Canada, compulsions upon the federal or a provincial government to call out the military are rare indeed. That is why the so-called "October Crisis" of 1970, which culminated in the assassination of Quebec's Labour Minister and Deputy Premier Pierre Laporte, plays so prominent a part in the literature.

It arose from the activities in and around Montreal of a small, amateurish, group whose members called themselves the Front de Libération du Québec.

On October 5, 1970, four gunmen identified later as members of the FLQ's "Liberation Cell" kidnapped British Trade Commissioner James Cross from his residence and held him until December 3, when lawyers arranged his release in return for the kidnappers being guaranteed a flight by Canadian military aircraft to Cuba.

On October 10, Pierre Laporte was abducted outside his home in the Montreal suburb of St. Lambert. Five days later thousands of troops were rushed to Montreal and other places in Quebec to give aid to the civil power.

At 4 a.m. on October 16, the federal government proclaimed the War Measures Act, suspended civil liberties and banned the FLQ (the Act was replaced on December 2 by the Public Order Act, which extended most of the provisions of its predecessor for five months).

By noon on October 16 more than 450 Quebec residents had been imprisoned without charge. Of them, fewer than 20 were convicted and most of those pleaded guilty to reduced charges in return for light sentences.

On October 17, the day following declaration of the War Measures Act, a "cell" of the FLQ announced the "execution" of Pierre Laporte. His body was found in the trunk of the car that had been used to abduct him. It had been abandoned within the precincts of the heavily guarded military base of St. Hubert not far from the Laporte residence.

On December 27, three suspects in the Laporte assassination were arrested in a farmhouse south of Montreal and a week later, on January 4, 1971, the armed forces' intervention came to an end.

Surveying that episode from the distance of 28 years, Pierre Trudeau's decision to call out the army and arrest hundreds of "suspects" who were never charged might be seen as over-reaction. The "threat" to public order was from a small group of Quebec nationalists. But at the time, I can testify that inhabitants of Montreal were alarmed.

For years, the FLQ had been associated with about 100 bombings in the city, some of them fatal. There was no reliable information to counter what we were being exposed to by FLQ "bulletins" from radio and television; the "threat" seemed real enough to us, and Trudeau's decision was welcomed, as far as I could tell, by a majority of Montrealers.

Nationalists, of course, took a different view. Pierre Vallières even suggested that from 1969 on, if the government "had really wanted to [it] could have dismantled the FLQ's amateurish organization." Instead, it "planted" agents so that it could "blame certain Québécois for the use of force."[1]

A more likely explanation rests in Trudeau's consuming hostility to nationalism of any kind, but particularly to Quebec nationalism.

Added to this, as Richard Gwyn noted in referring to a CBC interview on the topic with then cabinet minister Jean-Luc Pépin, was the fact that Trudeau and his coterie were executing their own kind of revolution, that of infiltrating francophones into the Canadian majority, and it was to that revolution, rather than simply to peace and order, that the FLQ posed a threat.

"We were bringing off a revolution," Pépin said. "We held the key posts [in Ottawa]. We were making the civil service bilingual. We were a well-organized group of revolutionaries, just like them, but working in a quite different way."[2]

That well-organized revolution culminated in 1981-2 with the monstrous trick that changed Canada's system of government to the Quebec model of centralized authority. It was not brought about democratically and it is still in place. No relief is in sight until the Canadian majority assembles the means to repeal the Charter and reassert its attachment to inherent freedom and responsibility under the common law.

In the context of security, the experience of the past thirty years shows the risks involved, even in peaceful Canada, of using the armed forces for purposes other than their basic duty of securing Canadian territory.

Aid to the civil power is part of that duty. It was fulfilled in confrontations with native Canadians at Oka. In a parliamentary democracy the civil power is paramount, and its legitimacy rests in the power being deputed to it by the people in free elections. It rests also on an assumption that, over time, the fluctuations of partisan victories and defeats will average out to carve a political path not so far from the centre as to reach an extreme.

Until thirty years ago, that had been Canada's history. Quebecers' political acumen in voting strategically yielded them effective control over the federal government and a resulting shift of material benefits to Quebec's advantage; the political direction might be left of centre but it was not extreme. Despite Lester Pearson's warning of potential dictatorship, that threat to democracy was not taken seriously.

It was the combination of Quebec-based majorities in the House of Commons and a prime minister from Quebec dedicated to revolutionary change that caused the damage. It was Canada's misfortune that the personality trait in which he saw himelf, in Richard Gwyn's phrase, as Single Combat champion, was suited to using the power of office to achieve his revolutionary aim.[3]

Ironically, the determination he displayed in the October Crisis, and which undoubtedly added both to his popularity at home and to his reputation abroad, also hardened the determination of his nationalist opponents and may well be viewed as one of two turning points in Quebec's voyage toward sovereignty.

The other was reached when he imposed the Charter over Quebec's objections.

Thus by a curious twist of fate, the man who chose not to join his country's fight against Nazism and who, as we have seen, shunned the military and starved it of funds, owes much of his reputation to his use of the military to quell "an apprehended insurrection."

That the "insurrection" was of dubious validity in retrospect does not alter the fact that he acted decisively, but neither does it alter the other fact that his action contributed to the growth of the nationalism he intended his action to defeat.

Yet the man whose career and personality, as well as the carefully constructed public image, epitomize the free thinking individual was himself confused by a conviction that the state's job was to cure society's ills.

When he was 74 he wrote that "the subject of law must be the individual human being; the law must permit the individual to fulfill himself or herself to the utmost."[4]

How appropriate, then, that the man who shunned armed service and treated defence matters with the neglect born of ignorance should also have been the one who didn't hesitate to call out the forces to aid the civil power in 1970. In that moment of crisis, the clouds cleared and he saw that keeping the peace was government's first duty.

Unfortunately for Canada, as soon as the crisis passed so did the clouds form again and eventually permeate the contradictory Charter. Nevertheless, the action Trudeau took without hesitation in 1970 set a precedent for circumstances at the turn of this century.

The decline in morale of Canada's armed forces, and its

reflection in the declining national morale I have tried to describe in the book, are the inevitable result of changing Canadians' perception of government.

No longer is it the referee that enforces rules to protect individuals' freedom from infringement; it has been turned into a paternalistic state that enters the field of play and misuses its force to equalize the outcomes of individuals exercising their different talents and capacities.

Individuals who formerly made their own decisions to get or spend and to abide by or break the law, are now assured that the paternalistic state will step in to aid them; all they have to do is to find the right sub-section of the law and one of the state's lawyers to argue for their entitlements.

More significantly, in the context of peace and order, is the Charter's encouraging *groups* of people, who think they are disadvantaged, to seek the state's intervention on their behalf.

When Ontario's labour union leaders staged their "days of protest" against the Harris government in 1996, they advertised the events as peaceful protests against that government's "failure to listen to us" and "fighting for the quality of life in this province."[5] But the real reason was the threat that the government's Bill 7 posed to the union leaders' power.

The legislation reversed what had been passed into law by the preceding Rae (NDP) government, whose legislation had banned the use of replacement workers during a legal strike, and added to unions' power a number of new rights. These were:

- the right to picket in shopping malls;
- first contract arbitration in case of bad faith bargaining;
- the right to organize certain categories of farm workers;
- restricting the right of employers to oppose certification applications; and
- strengthening the successor rights of unions when there was a transfer of ownership - the new owners must keep the union.

The Harris government's Bill 7 enacted revisions which ended the ban on replacement workers, removed successor rights, and required a mandatory vote in all union certifications (formerly, certification was automatic whenever 55 percent of employees could be persuaded to sign cards for union representation).

In chapter 2, we noted union leaders' expressed intentions to fight the new legislation. Later in the same year, before two "days of protest" were aimed at shutting down the city of Toronto, the Ontario Federation of Labour president said "Toronto is where the boss lives...and on October 25, we're going to throw him out of work. Toronto is the Mecca of the business community. It's the symbol of capitalism."[6]

In this sequence, two points are significant.

First is that the widespread picketing during the "days of protest" was illegal. None of the protesters was on strike and it is against the law to obstruct any person going about lawful affairs, such as entering a building.

Second is that union lawyers' arguments against injunctions to bar illegal picketing were based on precedents where Canadian courts interpreted the Charter's guarantees of freedom of expression and freedom of peaceful assembly as implying a right to picket.[7]

Peaceful assembly, I suggest, conveys a picture of people gathering in a public place, such as a park, or a hall rented for the purpose, or for that matter Parliament Hill in Ottawa, listening to speakers and parading their views for the attention of television cameras and the viewing audience.

Peaceful picketing on the other hand, which is lawful during a legal strike when workers have withdrawn their labour as part of the collective bargaining process, is done to explain their cause of grievance to other workers en route to work.

Usually those who are en route to work are either not members of the striking union or are members of management. The Supreme Court has ruled that the Charter's right to freedom of association includes the freedom not to associate.[8]

From this it would appear that once the peaceful picketers have informed a non-striking worker the cause of their grievance, their purpose has been served and they will make way for him.

In fact, the scene is anything but peaceful, and for this reason: the striking workers have been taught that the jobs they have walked away from are "their" jobs.

Even though the non-striking worker is going to his different job, it is not "his" job but a part of "theirs." If he is suspected of being a replacement worker, hired to do a job that a striking union member has vacated, he will be looked upon as a thief.

In short, the circumstances in which "peaceful" picketing lawfully occurs are conducive to strife.

The day before one of Toronto's "days of protest," the president of a union representing 7,600 Toronto Transit Commission workers said "I am recommending to our members that, for their own safety, they should not cross picket lines."[9]

At a meeting of union leaders to review those events, John Murphy, head of the Power Workers Union, spoke for many present when he said he didn't support blanket action because it offended public opinion. Instead, they would focus "on strikes and lockouts in which employers have taken advantage of Conservative labour laws to hire scabs."

Those who agreed with him planned to take a "more militant approach" by preventing substitute workers from going to work anywhere in the province. "If we have to physically stop them, we will," he said. "That's a focus that's much more militant, more effective than just walking up and down Bay Street."[10]

When strife occurs it is the duty of police to keep the peace. When strife occurs on picket lines, often the police will use their judgement, let the strife subside, and refrain from making arrests: legal strikes are a fact of life and after they are over life goes on. The hard feelings that strikes leave between strikers and non-striking co-workers are bad enough without bringing the law into it as well.

Different from this is picketing when the purpose is to show union leaders' power over their members by stopping *the public* from going about its lawful affairs; different because the purpose is to intimidate not only the public, but also the government that was elected by a majority of that same public.

Using force with the object of turning back legislation passed by the provincial parliament was somehow interpreted as being merely a part of normal day-to-day events, an offshoot of the grumbling about politics that goes on all the time.

To pretend that the setting up, at 300 public places, of groups of "protesters" drilled in the art of making nuisances of themselves could be described as peaceful assembly, was to deny the meaning of words.

From the events of those two days, certain impressions remain. On two occasions strikers were asked by a television reporter why they were picketing. Both of them said, "Because the union told me to."

On October 25, 1996, *The Globe and Mail* ran on its front page a photograph of a picket towering over a woman who wanted to go into the main postal depot to work. He was wearing a mask that covered his head, leaving only openings for the eyes and mouth. He was telling her that although she was free to leave the building, she wouldn't be allowed back in to do her work.

Union leaders who were interviewed, when they were asked the purpose of the protest, gave the same answer: it was to draw attention to the Harris government's cuts in social programs and the consequent damage to "working people."

Those same working people had been prevented from working that day because the unions' illegal action had shut down the TTC's buses and subway.

When Ann Bank tried to go to her place of work in the parliament buildings, after a two-and-a-half hour wait for a subway train that didn't come, she went home to get her car and drove to work where she was confronted by a picket line.

A female picket flung herself on the hood, claiming she had been hit. Ms. Bank was forced to wait for the five minutes dictated by the pickets to "inform" her why she was being stopped.

She switched off the engine and pointed out that there was no strike and she had the right to go to work, this, while surrounded by picketers who were soon joined "by a couple of dozen more." When the pickets relented they insisted she be stopped for another five minutes from the time she restarted her engine.

When she finally got to work she broke down. "Now I don't even know if the pickets will damage my car, or whether it will be towed, because I don't have parking privileges."[11]

None of the leaders made any connection with the federal government's cuts in transfer payments to Ontario, nor to successive federal governments' record of overspending and borrowing, nor to the plain fact that such borrowing, and the consequent call upon higher proportions of revenue to pay interest bills, meant a smaller proportion for social programs (the "poor") and interest paid to those who could afford to buy the government's bonds (the "rich").

In 1990, when Ontario's social democratic Rae government was elected, it faced an annual interest bill of $3.8 billion on a debt of $39.2 billion. Five years later, the annual interest bill was $8.6 billion on a debt of $97.5 billion.

In other words, the unacknowledged roots of the protest were in the years of union-inspired government extravagance which, instead of securing social programs, could not fail to weaken them. But in the leaders' words the protest was the familiar one against "the bosses," who were symbolized by Bay Street and the Toronto Stock

Exchange, both of which were targeted for demonstrations.

The irony appeared to be lost on union leaders. They represented their members, who were said to suffer from cuts in extravagant social programs that unions had urged on politicians for thirty years, but they also represented pension funds of which the top three alone had assets totalling $88 billion, much of the money invested in Canadian equities and debt securities through the financial institutions they were bad-mouthing.

All this was about attempts by union leaders to hang on to the power that changing conditions of trade and technology are wresting from their hands.

In Canada, the social democratic political influence of Quebec-dominated federal governments, and supported by the courts, has given labour unions power over "working people" that few politicians have the nerve to check.

They fear the loss of votes, but they also fear to be cast as encroaching upon the freedom of unions to deny freedom to others; they must appear to favour the collective over the individual in the socialist mode.

During discussions about the October protests the phrase that kept recurring in the mouths not only of union leaders but also of politicians belonging to the Liberal and New Democratic parties was that the Ontario government's actions to cut the province's deficit were "ideologically driven."

At the same time, voices of "working people" that were heard on radio and TV call-in programs drew parallels between the government's financial condition and their own.

One I heard was a single parent whose annual income was $27,000 and who had to manage her affairs carefully. She understood the reason for the cutbacks; what she resented was that the unions' action in shutting down public transport had cost her $25 to get to work that day; public transport she paid for, both at the wicket and through her taxes.

Those of the political left who were heard on the airwaves spoke of "the rich," of Ontario Premier "Mike Harris and his corporate friends," "the business community," "capitalism" and "the bosses" as if the class war they were waging (and the politics of envy they were practicing) were not ideologically driven at all.

A moment ago, we saw the irony of union leaders bad-mouthing the financial institutions that handled their pension funds' investments. Those funds illustrate the power of public sector unions to extract benefits from the system to build up funds far exceeding those of their union brothers in the private sector.

The list of the top 15 pension funds shows only two in the private sector, and both of those - Bell Canada Employees (No. 8) and Quebec Construction Workers (No. 15) - had strong links to government.

Total assets of the 13 public sector union funds were $160 billion. The top 5 were Ontario Teachers ($35 billion); Quebec Public Employees ($32 billion); Ontario Municipal Employees ($21 billion); Ontario Public Employees ($12 billion); and Alberta Public Employees ($9 billion).[12]

When that $160 billion total is set against the $300 billion that represented the total of all private pension fund assets, the power of collective bargaining to deprive the public of monopoly services is plain to see.

It has enabled one-sixth of the workforce to extract, also from the public, more than half as much as the private individuals who comprise the other five-sixths of the workforce were able to contribute to their own pension funds.

Small wonder the "days of protest" in Ontario were dominated by members of public sector unions.

If there is one thing that distinguishes countries that have reduced the power of unions over their workforces, it is the gains they achieved in productivity and employment afterwards. One form or another of their "right to work" laws entitle workers to work, and employers to employ them, without those workers having to join, or pay dues to, a union.

In New Zealand after such laws were enacted in 1991, when unemployment was 10.9 percent, by 1995 the rate had fallen to 6.1 percent. In US states with such laws, manufacturing employment increased by 148 percent between 1947 and 1992 compared to barely measurable growth in other states.[13]

Margaret Thatcher's long battle with, and eventual victory over, the militants in Britain's unions played a leading part in that country's economic recovery. As she put it in her memoirs: "What the [National Union of Miners] strike's defeat established was that Britain could not be made ungovernable by the Fascist Left."[14]

Mention of the Fascist Left reminds us that the militancy of Canada's public sector unions in 1996 was aimed at a freely elected government, categorized as "the employer," that was also categorized as "capitalist." Socialism, which always involves coercion, fits naturally into the aims of militant unionists who want their ally, the state, to dominate society.

It would be comforting to think that Canadians' characteristic politeness and tolerance were proof against the urgings of extremists. But history shows that given deteriorating economic conditions, civility also deteriorates, and demagogues declaim against selected oppressors at the cost of public order.

History also shows that demagogues always choose an enemy to divert their followers' attention from the real cause of the circumstances they rail against.

None of this makes cheerful reading. Union leaders and the social activists who flocked to join them were quick to claim that the crowd that marched on the provincial parliament building was a broadly based "social movement" that would spread across the country.

Yet the complaint that appeared to unite them was that Canada's thirty-year growth of state intrusion into the people's lives was finally receding under the weight of debt and its accompanying drag upon the creation of wealth.

Wealth was identified with rich people, the capitalists of socialist lore, rather than with the healthy, productive society that could emerge when people were free to act in their own interests, provided they did not restrict or in any way infringe upon the freedom of others to do the same.

Representative government in Canada has been distorted for thirty years by a malignant combination: presence within the state of a consistently socialistic regime in Quebec; and control of the federal government by ministers from Quebec steeped in the same philosophy.

Thus has Canada been trapped in decline. Socialism has prevented Quebec from realizing its potential; socialism has damaged Canada's own economy while suffering the seepage of wealth to sustain a declining Quebec.

No remedy is in sight so long as the combination persists.

But this does not mean that representative government has failed; certainly not that it should be replaced by the thinly veiled mobocracy of a union-led "social movement."

In fact until the 1960s, Canada worked surprisingly well despite Quebec's reluctance to modernize its institutions, largely because governments confined themselves to governing, and practiced fiscal rectitude.

The rot started with Pearson and Trudeau wrecking the federal system by imposing "universal" health and other programs whose unrecognized costs outran revenues and began the upward spiral of deficits and debt. Yet in 1996, Prime Minister Chrétien was brazen enough to blame the debt burden on two Mulroney governments that were dealt the mess by Liberal predecessors in which Chrétien served as finance minister.

The threat to representative government was expressed by the extremists who led the days of protest. Under the sub-title Toronto Direct Action Committee, a picket sign of the Ontario Coalition Against Poverty read "City By City Is Way Too Slow. Let's Shut Down ONTARIO!"

Pat Clancy, vice-president of the Labour Council of Metropolitan Toronto, said "We will have that general strike, and we have proved today that we can do it."

Canadian Auto Workers President Buzz Hargrove said: "This is a first in Toronto, but there will be more across the province. And the entire province and country is going to be shut down at some point. I would predict within the next year and a half."[15]

He described the day of protest as a "wonderful expression of democracy for us. People are out saying, 'We do not accept that democracy means voting once every four years and turning over the total responsibility for the social, economic and political agenda of this province to a group of 82 people'... People are here today saying, 'We're not going to accept a government that is just governing for the people on Bay St. We're entitled to have input. We're going to keep demanding it until we get it.'"[16]

Such revolutionary sentiments were nowhere to be heard while Ontario's previous Liberal and NDP governments almost tripled the province's debt in 10 years. Union leaders' opposition to their socialist brothers was restricted to the NDP's efforts to reduce the rate of growth in the government's wage bill.

Mr. Hargrove's claim that the well organized display of illegal acts was "a wonderful expression of democracy" only draws our attention to the display.

All the picketing was illegal, yet the police condoned their union brothers' illegal acts by agreeing with picket captains that fellow citizens going about their lawful affairs would be stopped from doing so for only five minutes.

How many citizens, especially women and older people, stayed home rather than face angry pickets? How many who braved the pickets were insulted or hustled? How many paid taxi fare to get to work because the TTC was shut down by the brute force of illegal picketing? How many suffered fates similar to that of Ms. Bank? How many union brothers were bused in from New York and Michigan to break the law in Canada?

Representative democracy enables the citizens to elect representatives to the ancient institution of Parliament. Once there, a majority forms the government of the day, but in each riding, and regardless of party affiliation, the elected member speaks for all the citizens.

Granted, the distortion imposed by caucus discipline will force MPs to toe party lines, nevertheless, in the personal concerns that trouble individual citizens their MP will seek redress through the bureaucracy.

In due course, as we said before, voters' opinions change, governing majorities change too, and over the years a middle course is followed. The polarization that has occurred in Canada is due to the peculiar circumstances of Quebec's strategic votes, a divided opposition that assures Liberal victories in vote-rich Ontario, and the resulting control by the political left.

As an aside, the actions by Mr. Hargrove and his followers reinforce the conclusions reached by Barbara Kulaszka: the media-dubbed "far-right" is on the fringe and ineffectual; it is the far-left that not only threatens the peace but breaks it with impunity.

In Canada's representative democracy it is open to union leaders to join, or to form, a political party and run for office. If they want to change the system, that is the way to set about it. If they object to the idea of the secret ballot, as they have done strenuously for their own members in the matter of letting them see employers' offers and voting on acceptance or rejection, they will be free as MPs to advocate that in Parliament.

In other words, instead of subjecting the listening and viewing public to single issue tirades, and basking in the resultant publicity, they would be members of Parliament and subject to the rules of debate they scorn today.

But that would also bring them within the scope of long established procedures they are dedicated to overthrowing.

It may be too far a stretch, in peaceful Canada, to remind ourselves that although Karl Marx thought that the spread of the franchise would make revolution possible without violence, Lenin reinterpreted Marx's thought.

Once in power he defined the dictatorship of the proletariat as "rule based upon force and unrestricted by any laws." He also changed the meaning of revolution to mean, exclusively, a *violent* rise to power.[17]

It may be too far a stretch, but the parallel is there and history shows that threats to peace are rooted in the political left.

It follows that, as I suggested before, the armed forces' experience in "peacekeeping" abroad, and which I also suggested has been at odds with training for national defence, may yet fit into Canada's needs at home.

Accordingly it is appropriate to review a recent instance when that experience, called upon in Somalia, revealed a breakdown in co-operation between political leaders and the armed forces.

Such co-operation is essential if the combination is to work in keeping the peace in Canada.

Chapter 9

The Somalia Inquiry - a national disgrace

Co-operation as a principle of war is such a pervasive requirement that it is apt to be taken for granted. Political co-operation between allies of Western democracies in the face of a common threat to their freedoms is as necessary as it is, if war occurs, between their armed forces.

Where co-operation is just as important, and where attaining it is far harder, is in peacetime, both between allies and between the components of their separate forces.

In peacetime, democratic governments suffer the push and pull of competing interests. The wars that appear on television screens are remote. Even if one's own country's forces are engaged in "peacekeeping", it is peace that is being kept: the need to spend large sums of taxpayers' money on "defence" is neither apparent nor attractive.

Nevertheless the necessity of the defence function is recognized. Where co-operation becomes paramount is in the determination, within the limits of straitened defence budgets, of how the money is to be spent.

Manufacturers press their wares; politicians press the claims of their constituencies; soldiers, sailors and airmen press the needs of their respective services. But above the fray stand the principles of war.

The aim is to defend Canada's territorial integrity. If the armed forces that are designed for that purpose are also called upon for lesser tasks, they will adapt their weapons and logistics to such lesser purposes. But not the other way around.

No one knows what kind of war might threaten Canada's territorial integrity in the future. It would be folly to tailor its armed forces to the demands of "peacekeeping" in countries that pose no threat to Canada.

If Canada were to enter a "hot" war, its land, sea and air forces would need all the individual courage and resourcefulness for which the Canadian armed services are renowned. Above all, they would need full and unstinted co-operation among all three arms of the services in order to prevail.

It is in peacetime, when a capacity to stand above the conflicting interests is as vital an attribute of statesmen as it is of military leaders, that co-operation is essential.

It would be hard to find a more graphic illustration of that capacity's absence from the Canadian scene than in the circumstances surrounding the Somalia Inquiry of 1995-7.

It was established by then defence minister David Collenette, in March 1995, to investigate incidents that occurred during the deployment of Canadian Joint Forces Somalia two years before - a successful, though necessarily limited operation designed to bring some sort of order to a country in an advanced state of anarchy.

Canada was one of 23 nations supplying soldiers, sailors and airmen to the US-led United Task Force Somalia during *Operation Deliverance* from December 13, 1992 to May 31, 1993.

The united forces totalled 49,535 personnel to which the US was the major contributor with 30,317. Canada's complement of 1,360 consisted of HMCS *Preserver*, a Canadian Airborne Regiment Battle Group, and an Airlift Control Element, supported by the corresponding staff formations.

Preserver, stationed off Somalia, housed the force's headquarters until HQ was relocated in the coastal city of Mogadishu, the capital; and then in Belet Huen, also on the coast some 160 miles north of Mogadishu. *Preserver* did double duty as a Rest and Recreation post for troops, and its Sea Kings flew supplies ashore for the Airborne Regiment.[1]

The Airlift Control Element had already been in operation from September 10, 1992 to October 27, 1992, when it accomplished the Canadian government's undertaking to airlift food and other supplies into southern Somalia under *Operation Relief*. This was achieved by an air transport detachment from 427 Sqn. that reached a peak of 6 Hercules flying out of Nairobi. The other air element in the joint force was the 93rd Rotary Wing Flight at Belet Huen.

Three Hercules of the Airlift Control Element were dedicated to ferrying people and supplies to and from Nairobi to sustain the Airborne. Everything from rations to drinking water, fresh fruit, ammunition, medical supplies and mail had to be flown in daily. (The alternative - overland from Mogadishu - was across country where roads were marked on maps as "heavily mined" and two Canadian armoured vehicles were blown up.)

Standard procedure on arrival at Belet Huen was a reconnaissance of the 5,670-foot gravel airstrip to check for camels and donkeys on the runway. Landings were "maximum effort" using full reverse and braking. As the huge dustball from the reversing props advanced, reverse was pulled back to keep the engine intakes clear of it until the aircraft reached the even dustier off-loading area at the end of the runway.

But at least the aircrews would fly back to Nairobi, unlike their compatriots in Belet Huen who were obliged to "munch on dreary rations before bedding down under canvas with their regular night-time companions - scorpions and huge camel spiders."[2]

Participating nations were authorized, under UN Security Council Resolution 794, to use whatever force was necessary to protect allied forces, Somali nationals, and the employees of non-governmental organizations (NGOs), as well as their related matériel, from hostile forces in the region.

These consisted of gunmen, bandits, warlords, and "technicals," whose name derived from the "technical assistance" expense vouchers issued by UN and relief agencies and intended for famine victims. Instead they were misappropriated by the well-armed locals (supplying "protection") who drove around the wrecked towns and cities of Somalia in jeeps and small trucks, looting and killing at random.

Somalia, with a 1,700-mile coastline, covers the Horn of Africa from the north, where it forms the south shore of the Gulf of Aden; to the south-east, where its western border with Kenya meets the Indian Ocean about 2 degrees south of the Equator. Kenya's capital, Nairobi, is about 675 miles from Mogadishu.

Somalia is roughly the shape of a figure 7, with the eastern wedge of Ethiopia inserted below the bar of the seven and along Kenya's northern border. The wedge is the Ogaden, peopled largely by Somalis, which was the scene of fighting in 1977-8. Ethiopia fought Somali rebels that it claimed were armed and reinforced by Somali troops.

It was Soviet support of Ethiopia that led Somalia to expel Russian troops from Somalia, and the next year Soviet-armed Cuban troops defeated ethnic Somalis and Somali troops in Ethiopia. As many as 1.5 million refugees entered Somalia. There was a prolonged drought followed by years of widespread violence and clan warfare (there are at least 20 clans and sub-clans and as many factions) during which some 2 million people were displaced.

In 1992 the estimated population of Somalia was 8,000,000, about one-third urban, two-thirds rural. Normal daytime temperatures range between 35 and 45 degrees C., rising to 50 and above in April and May. Humidity ranges from 60 to 80 percent. A quarter of the land is desert. Highlands in the north, which reach to 8,000 feet, give way to plateaus and lowlands to the south, much of the land savanna.

By the time the US Marines landed on the beach at Mogadishu in December 1992, almost all Somali institutions had collapsed in the prevailing anarchy. Throughout southern Somalia, clan and factional warfare, extortion, banditry, and indiscriminate shooting had displaced hundreds of thousands of people and destroyed the economy, the security and the health services.

This was a country *in extremis*, lawless, controlled by armed gangs, with no stores, gas stations, banks or schools, no electricity, no running water, no garbage collection and no sewers. Houses and other buildings looted, windows broken, almost every family bereaved, food scarce or unobtainable, money and valuables long exhausted - and nowhere to go because everywhere was the same.[3]

Canada's soldiers saw a country bleeding to death from self-inflicted wounds. Completely lacking among Somali men was the instinctive Canadian attitude, when confronted with difficulty, of everyone pitching in to help. But in Somalia it was the reverse. Somali males would do nothing voluntarily, rather would they watch Canadians doing the work and take it as a matter of course.

In Somalia, it was women's place to do the heavy work. At a roadblock, Canadian soldiers who were searching for guns unloaded a truck carrying bags of rice, but when the Somali men were told to reload, they turned to their women. Outraged, the Canadians ordered the Somali men to work at gunpoint.[4]

The condition of the country when the Canadians arrived was the outcome of the civil war that began four years before in 1988. Although one of the two main warring parties was defeated in May 1992, and its leader exiled, the fighting continued as other factions splintered and fought for control.

Mogadishu was divided by a no-man's-land roughly six blocks wide that ran north to south through the city, separating the two major factions of the United Somali Congress, one led by Mohammed Farrah Aideed and the other by Ali Mahdi Mohammed. This line could only be crossed at great risk and by paying bribes.

Aideed controlled the port and the airfield, both of which came under fire from Mahdi's forces. This crippled relief efforts. Only one ship was able to dock between September and November 1992. Two relief ships were fired on and had to turn away, another was shelled and ran aground, where it burned.[5]

Kismayu, the other major seaport in southern Somalia, was controlled by another faction led by Ahmed Omar Jess, who charged exorbitant fees for access to it. Inland, other factions sustained themselves by raiding the countryside and stealing or extorting supplies from relief agencies. As many as 14 major factions fought for territory and influence, themselves split further into smaller factions fighting each other.

In Mogadishu, according to hospital records, the daily violent death toll was over 150; how many died away from the hospitals is unknown. CARE estimated that one quarter of the Somali population under five years of age had vanished - a lost generation.

Food was a weapon for survival and power. The relief agencies became the targets of the people they were trying to help. Typical was a food convoy of 25 trucks outward bound from Mogadishu to Baidoa and Oddur. Five of the trucks were extorted as the price for permission to leave the city; 12 were hijacked en route; eight reached Baidoa only to be looted there. No food reached the intended recipients.

Even after Canada's airlift delivered relief supplies - an impressive 4,000 metric tons a week - many of the trucks that were loaded never reached the warehouse a few kilometres from the airfield.

Everything of value that survived the civil war was stolen and sold or bartered for cash or services: electrical wire for its copper; sewer and fresh water pipes pulled from the ground; roads holed to slow vehicles so that they could be looted.

In 1992, over 150 UN 4-wheel-drive Toyota pickups, which were especially prized by "technicals," were hijacked.[6]

Restoring order was a matter of Canadian soldiers forcing their Bisons, Grizzlies and Cougars across rugged terrain, beset by damage from "wait-a-bit" thorns or landmines, in temperatures between 100 and 130 degrees F., and with the wind whirling dust-devils like tornadoes, sometimes through tents and equipment, coating everything with dust. "The night belongs to local thieves."[7]

This was the situation that faced the Unified Task Force in December 1992.

Canadian Joint Forces Somalia began operation on December 28, 1992, when the first elements of the Canadian Airborne Regiment Battle Group reached Belet Huen to restore order in an area - known as the Humanitarian Relief Sector (HRS) - which soon, with the arrival of supply ships, was extended over 30,000 square kilometres.

The Canadian approach from the first day was to co-operate with the NGOs and local groups by asking them what they wanted CJFS to do for them. That same night, the Airborne saturated the town of Belet Huen with foot patrols to show that they were responsible for security.

The next day CJFS met with the tribal kings and elders to emphasize that the Canadian presence was temporary and it was up to them, the traditional leaders, to find Somali solutions to Somali problems.

Within two months, banditry was eradicated: Canada's HRS was the first in the United Task Force to be declared secure. As a result, CJFS found itself escorting major relief convoys well outside the HRS boundaries. UNITAF's commander, US Lieutenant General Robert B. Johnston, said "there was no mission the Canadians wouldn't accept."

In line with the policy of encouraging Somalis to help themselves, many of the Airborne's 50-strong medical staff did voluntary work in the local Belet Huen hospital throughout the period.

World Food Program representatives in Mogadishu were persuaded to provide food for Belet Huen's volunteer policemen, and by the time CJFS left, the town's police force had grown from 150 to 350, with some 100 more in villages of the HRS.

All had been issued with uniforms, were paid monthly by a UN agency, and were administered by the Airborne. They were trained in first aid and riot control until they were qualified to be issued with firearms - 30 Beretta rifles that the Airborne had confiscated during weapons searches.

In Belet Huen CJFS formed a Reconstruction/Rehabilitation Committee and persuaded UN representatives in Mogadishu to monetize some of the allotted aid. This was then administered by the Airborne to pay daily labourers working on infrastructure reconstruction.

Roads and bridges were repaired and UNICEF was persuaded to second educational experts for the testing, selection, and retraining of former teachers. One school was repaired, then three others. April 8, 1993, was the first time in 24 months that secular schools had operated in the Belet Huen area.

With help and supervision by the Airborne, villages in the HRS were able to reopen their schools as well.

Belet Huen's four schools were accommodating more than 6,000 children, and a milestone was passed when the local Somali educational authority proposed, on its own initiative, the establishment of vocational training for adults at night. CJFS supplied the generators and wiring for two of the schools.

The outcome of all this activity was self-evident: markets flourished; yards were swept; garbage was burnt; latrines were dug and covered; new buildings were built and others repainted. The Oxford Institute of Languages and Science at the east end of Belet Huen was joined by the Vancouver Institute, also specializing in the arts and sciences.

On May 31, 1993, when CJFS left Belet Huen after handing over to Germans, Italians, and Nigerians, its commanding officer felt the Canadians had built confidence not only between themselves and the Somalis, but also between the clans: that the force's efforts were leaving a legacy of peace and stability.[8]

That the legacy was of short duration was evidenced by a report three years later that Somali warlords had declared an end to hostilities "in their devastated country" at the end of a week of talks at the invitation of Kenyan President Daniel arap Moi.

Free movement of people would be permitted in Mogadishu and all roadblocks would be removed. The Kenyan President "appealed to the Somali leaders to consider that for the last six years Somalia has had no internationally recognized government and that there has been a lot of suffering by the Somali people, especially women and children."[9]

Only two months later, the warlords were at it again: in five days of a widening battle for Mogadishu, 135 people had been killed and 900 wounded.[10]

The Canadian Airborne Regiment did a professional job in shocking circumstances that should have enhanced the proud tradition born at Anzio and in Normandy fifty years before. Instead it ran foul not so much of disciplinary failure as of trying to conceal the crime that was committed.

That soldiers, whose profession is to fight and if necessary die for a cause, should be redesigned overnight as policemen and civil engineers was bad enough.

That they should be sent to keep the peace between well-armed, mobile, and bloodthirsty thugs in a war-ravaged country devoid of any significance to Canada's defence or national interests was even worse.

But that recriminations from the attempted cover-up should not only be used to justify disbanding the regiment but should be stretched out, four years after the event, into a political drama of national proportions - that is a disgrace.

The bare facts are that on March 4, 1993, a Somali infiltrator to the CJFS base at Belet Huen, Ahmed Afraraho Aruush, was shot and killed by a Canadian sentry. On March 16, 1993, Somali national Shidane Omar Arone was caught sneaking into the base. Later that night, while in custody, he was beaten to death.

Although a press release stated that a Somali had died in custody, it was issued in Mogadishu, 160 miles away, and Canadian journalists arriving in Belet Huen were not told about it, nor was it copied to NDHQ in Ottawa (however, then defence minister Kim Campbell said her staff heard of the incident on March 17).

On March 19, a corporal of the Airborne who had been taken into custody in connection with the second Somali's death, tried to hang himself. At a news conference the Airborne CO confirmed the attempted suicide but refused to say why the corporal was in custody, did not link that to the second Somali's death, nor did he say that the deaths occurred.[11]

Yet it was neither the breakdown of discipline that led to the murder and the corporal's attempted suicide, nor the foolish attempts to cover up afterwards, that caused the Defence Minister to disband the Airborne Regiment in 1995. What horrified him and the Prime Minister was publication in the press of excerpts from two amateur videos.

One included soldiers of the regiment using coarse language; the other showed soldiers taking part in repulsive hazing rituals. The last straw was that the coarse language included the dreaded "N" word, and the concomitant suspicion that the soldier who uttered it was nothing less than a racist.

This pathetic performance by a minister of the Crown was distinguished by a singular ignorance of the nuts and bolts of his job.

The Canadian Airborne Regiment was not an infantry regiment of the regular kind exemplified by the Royal 22nd (the Van Doos), or the Princess Patricia's Canadian Light Infantry (the PPCLIs). It was composed of members of such regular regiments who volunteered for service in the Canadian Airborne and who still belonged to those regiments while serving in the Airborne. After their tour of duty with the Airborne ended, they returned to their regiments.

This process had two objectives: first, to shield the Airborne from the perils of "elitism"; that is, the folly of thinking you're better than anyone else because you belong to a particular group; and second, to expose the regiment, and professional airborne doctrine, to the new ideas, and new ways of doing things, that result from bringing in new people.

This didn't mean that it wasn't an honour to volunteer, and be selected, for service with the Airborne; it was. Jumping out of aircraft is a dangerous business. Jumping out loaded with full kit under enemy fire knowing that you're going to be in action the moment you hit the ground is a business for heroes. Men who returned to their regiments wearing the coveted paratrooper's wing had something to say for themselves.

Disbanding the Airborne was not only a shameful thing to do; it was also a mistake. The men who appeared on the videos were not only unrepresentative; some had already either returned to their parent regiments or left the service.

Except for the few who were directly involved, the corporate whole of the Airborne that Jean Chrétien and David Collenette disbanded was innocent of the "crimes" that so alarmed the Liberals' sensitivity.

The disciplinary failures at Belet Huen were traceable to other failures within the regiment when it was at Petawawa *before* it went to Somalia.

By choosing to disband the whole regiment, the politicians showed two things: first, their ignorance of the military structure; and second, their ignorance of the fundamentals of discipline: you don't punish a unit, you punish the individuals who let the unit down.

Morale, as I mentioned before, is a state of mind, especially of persons associated in some enterprise, with reference to confidence, courage, hope, zeal, etc.

It is also fragile. Readers who served in the armed forces will recall instances when they could tell the state of a unit's morale the moment they crossed the threshold of a ship, an army base, or an air force station.

Commanders lead by example. In war at the unit level they take part in hazardous engagements as a matter of course; senior commanders who did the same in their day practice leadership by exercising the characteristics that command respect: honesty, integrity, professional competence, fairness and self-discipline.

None of this is easy. Factors that contribute to its decline can be identified from experience. The airman's guide to self-preservation - "If it moves, salute it; if it doesn't, paint it white" - carries more than a grain of truth. Part of discipline is pride in appearance, of things as well as people.

Attention to detail may sound tedious but it also contributes to getting it right the first time. Completing tasks in sequence, rather than tackling the easy ones first, gets them all done expeditiously. Issuing orders that are clear, and making sure that they are understood, will secure compliance. Obeying orders once they have been issued is vital.

Once slippage is allowed to occur in any of those factors, morale suffers.

A commander's first duty is always to the men he leads. The moment they suspect he is putting himself and his own interests first, he forfeits their respect. If they don't respect him, they are less likely to obey orders without question, less likely to respect immediate superiors who are associated with the commander, less likely to take pride in their work and their appearance, less likely to be proud of the unit in which they serve.

This does not mean that an ill-disciplined formation will not contain well-disciplined units. Leaders arise at all levels and will insist on maintaining within the unit the high standards they set themselves.

Maintaining discipline in the conditions that faced our soldiers in Somalia could not have been easy. The results they achieved despite those conditions do credit to their training and dedication to duty. Nevertheless the breakdown of discipline that culminated in the murder reflected on the commander of the Airborne at the time and to a lesser degree on the commander of CJFS. But blame did not stop there.

Morale is a state of mind. It comprises confidence, courage, hope, zeal, etc., but among the *et cetera* is loyalty.

Loyalty works both ways. It begins at the smallest unit, the platoon, flight or section, where corporals, sergeants and junior officers owe and practice loyalty to one another in their duty to care for the men and women under command.

Care implies seeing that they are fed, clothed, and housed as well as can be done with the resources available at the time and place of service: seeing that they get their mail; seeing, too, that personal problems can be confided to someone they know from experience, or from the experience of their comrades, will lend an ear and try to help them.

At the level of battalion, small ship, or squadron, the commander leads by example but he depends also on his junior officers to keep him posted. He trusts them to run their affairs, but he also trusts them to tell him when trouble is brewing that he ought to know about.

Enforcement of discipline through arrest, charge, and adjudication, works the same way. Minor offences are dealt with on the spot by verbal admonition.

If they are repeated, or if there are distinct breaches of the law, a charge is laid and the offender is paraded before his officer, who hears the evidence and decides whether to dismiss the charge, or to make a summary award of punishment within the scope of his authority.

If the charge is serious, and the evidence is compelling, he remands it to his superior; but at that level, even though the unit or formation commander has the authority to make a summary award, the accused has the right (and must be told that he has the right) to elect trial by court-martial, where he will be defended by an officer appointed for the purpose; or, just as in civilian life, he can hire a lawyer at his own expense, or apply for legal aid.

Loyalty moves both ways, down from commanders to those they command, but also up through the whole chain, through the chiefs of staffs of the three services to the chief of defence staff to the minister of defence to the prime minister to the monarch.

In our monarchical system, loyalty is to the monarch who represents no party or faction but all the people of Canada.

In practice, the monarch is remote, but the tradition she represents is enduring. It is one of inherent freedom and responsibility under the evolving common law that antedates Magna Carta. Defending that tradition is the sum of her armed forces' duty to her and to the people of Canada.

The armed forces are funded, and their terms of service are determined, by the government of the day, and they owe it the loyalty of servant to master in the practical way that civilian workers owe loyalty to their employers. But the loyalty that goes beyond practical ways, and that inspires soldiers, sailors and airmen to put their necks on the line, is to the idea of freedom that the Queen represents.

This, the readiness if necessary to die for an idea raises armed service above the push and pull of politics and above the self-interest that infuses party and faction.

At one time, the men who served in the British and Canadian forces were so insulated from politics that the topic, by tradition and common consent, was one of three banned from discussion in officers' messes and wardrooms; the other two topics were religion and women.

All three were private matters. Discussing them could lead only to division and hostility among men whose motive was to support one another in a higher cause.

That the cause was patriotism, or love of country and what it stood for, brings us to Dr. Johnson and the often mistaken meaning of his celebrated remark: "Patriotism is the last refuge of a scoundrel."

When Johnson said it, Jean-Jacques Rousseau was propagating his idea of the General Will that was fulfilled in the French Revolution (and much later in the twentieth century horrors of Lenin, Hitler, Stalin, Mao Tse-tung and Pol Pot) - the idea that the will of the people must prevail.

The trick was that the General Will turned out to be not general at all, because they who had the political power took care that it was *their* will that prevailed.

According to Rousseau, the General Will would be embodied in the State, to which the people would owe lives that would be shaped by social engineering to conform with the (undefined) General Will. The State was the father, it represented the fatherland, *la patrie*, and that, the *patriotism* of socio/cultural engineering, was what Johnson detested.

So when we speak of loyalty reaching up the line through the chiefs of staff to the defence minister and the prime minister, we are confronted again with the conflict between the two modes of thought we mentioned earlier.

The politician seeks vagueness in which he and his colleagues can escape their critics. The soldier requires precise direction so that the orders he must give in turn can be precise.

But when, as in Canada, the system of government was turned through 180 degrees, not only did the politician's role change, but the soldier's understanding of his own role was turned too.

When government's whole emphasis was changed from one of free individuals taking responsibility for their own lives and actions, to a completely different one, wherein a political class declared the people's dependency upon the state - as in Rousseau's General Will - so did the soldier's attitude change as well.

Before, the soldier was subject to military discipline that was stricter than were civilian penalties for infringement of the common law, but he shared with civilians the freedom to make his own decisions about behaviour.

After Canada's conversion into a paternalistic welfare state, and its embodiment in a radically changed Constitution, the soldier was told that, like his civilian neighbour, he had certain rights that were "guaranteed" to him by the Canadian state.

He was less a soldier under orders, and more of a civilian who happened to be in uniform; less a soldier within the complex and extended family of his service, and more of a civilian in uniform entitled to certain benefits and rights he could claim, at law, if necessary.

Accompanying this changing attitude were the changes imposed upon the military establishment: unification; bilingualism; cuts in funding and personnel; seemingly endless making do with outdated equipment; above all, disbandment of the separate service headquarters dedicated to army, navy and air force, and their replacement by a "unified" bureaucracy in which senior officers vied with their civilian counterparts for rank and position.

Add to this, the built-in confusion between two separate kinds of activity - fighting to protect Canada, and "peacekeeping" in countries that are remote from Canada - and then put yourself in the boots of a young Canadian sentry, trained in those two conflicting roles, on a dark night with the hot wind blowing, in a lawless country where the whole atmosphere is hostile, and ask yourself what you might have done when you saw that infiltrator to the camp you were guarding?

When during its protracted deliberations we saw the Somalia Inquiry fussing about the way senior officers manipulated the department's responses to journalists' requests for information, who could avoid comparing them to the way politicians have done the same thing for years?

How many readers and viewers recalled the rumours surrounding the bidding up of prices when private oil companies were bought out to form PetroCanada, or the rumours of "commissions" that facilitated the sale of Candu reactors - and the blank walls of cabinet secrecy that kept investigative journalists at bay then and since?

How many remembered the start of the decline 30 years before when Members of Parliament voted themselves a 50 percent raise, a 33 percent increase in non-taxable allowances, and a fully-indexed pension scheme beyond the reach of the constituents they were elected to serve?

More recently, how many were reminded of electoral promises unkept; and of a deputy prime minister's prevarication, reluctant resignation, and shameless re-election at great expense to the public?

To cap all this, when the Somalia Inquiry came too close to involving prominent members of the political class (and this not long before the Prime Minister's calling of a general election) the inquiry was hastily shut down.

Morale is fragile, and loyalty works both ways. Critics of Canada's armed forces need to look beyond Somalia to a fatal flaw in the Canadian *political* establishment. Just as successful military leaders command respect by personal example, so have Canada's political leaders failed to acquire, even to understand the need for, that quality.

Prime ministers who brag abroad about the merits of the country they are supposed to lead, are markedly less attentive to the needs of the men and women at home whose dedication to *service* is that same country's safeguard.

Chapter 10

Summing up

The theme of this book has been the influence upon Canada's development, and upon its armed forces, of a thirty-year subjection to statist policies that originated in Quebec and have steadily eroded the British tradition of the Canadian majority.

The mistaken idea that enlightened governors can manage something so intricate and varied as a provincial economy came as naturally to the social democrats who led Quebec's Quiet Revolution as it did to the "Three Wise Men" Lester Pearson imported from Quebec to advise him about the political economy of Canada.

The revolution that Jean-Luc Pépin spoke of, and which was threatened by the FLQ, was inseparable from the statist philosophy of the French tradition.

The fundamental difference between the two outlooks is found in understandings of freedom.

The French tradition stems from Rousseau, the French Revolution, and the idea that freedom depends upon law that protects the individual by guaranteeing certain defined, and therefore limited, rights. That law, as Canada's Charter of Rights and Freedoms declares, is supreme.

The British tradition, on the other hand, stems from the idea of inherent freedom and responsibility: each one is duty bound to uphold both the law and the free institutions that sustain a self-governing society.

In the French tradition, the individual's freedom is limited to the rights that the law defines and that the government, as enforcer of the law, permits. In Pierre Trudeau's words, "the subject of law must be the individual human being; the law must permit the individual to fulfill himself or herself to the utmost."

When those two different understandings are applied to methods of government, the distinction is evident.

The French method inclines the citizen to look upon himself as a free-standing individual, guaranteed that status by his government, jealous of what the law permits him to do and, secure within the government's protection and the law's permission, content to let his governors do the rest.

As French author and diplomat Alain Peyrefitte wrote: "We

leave it to the state to care for our happiness - and reproach it for not making us happy enough. We beg from it what we are unwilling to obtain for ourselves - and snarl at it for not giving it to us, or not giving us enough of it, or fast enough."[1]

The British method calls upon the individual to exercise his inherent freedom within the bounds of an equal responsibility to respect the freedom of others and to uphold the free institutions that have developed since Anglo-Saxon times.

The French method, which imputes to man the ability to define the individual's rights in such a way as to secure his freedom, runs foul of time and chance. What seemed to be a good thing to guarantee at one time, loses favour at a later time. But to change the written supreme law is not done either easily or gradually. Alain Peyrefitte again: "In our French hierarchical system, rights are either unilaterally bestowed and thus revocable, or else they are wrested violently from the state or the privileged and so threatened by counter-violence."[2]

By contrast, the British method recognizes that times change, and we change with them. The common law that citizens are expected to uphold was not written down for all time, but is a living body made from judgements decided by judges and juries in particular cases that were, and are, brought before the courts.

The two methods represent two lines of thought: the French is Utopian, seeking man's perfectibility through man-made decrees; the British is worldly, recognizing that man is imperfect but still ready to do the best he can for himself and society.

The worldly approach is by definition practical, but it also recognizes that perfection is not of this world. The words of the hymn *O worship the King* remind us that:

> The earth with its store of wonders untold,
> Almighty, Thy power hath founded of old;
> Hath stablish'd it fast by a changeless decree,
> And round it hath cast, like a mantle, the sea.

Changeless decrees are the prerogative of the Almighty.

From these observations we can infer the likelihood of different outcomes from the two methods.

The French is man-made, fixed in the time the decrees were written, hard to change, and therefore vulnerable to the effect of new ideas. Because it was made by men who later are thought to have been wrong, it will have to be overturned by other men who think they are right (Pierre Trudeau remarked in 1977 that the French had

had 17 constitutions in 170 years).

The British method, also man-made, accepts that times change, but that defending the individual's inherent freedom is a continuing responsibility and a personal one. It is also a responsibility he shares with the monarch who personifies the tradition.

This last, the personal link to a monarch, distinguishes the British method not only from the French but also from the republican that characterizes both France and the United States of America.

It is a curious thing that Canadians who, however well disposed they might be toward their American neighbours, are quick to affirm their preference for Canada, affirm also their attachment to a Canada which "includes Quebec." Yet the French method that Quebec exemplifies is as contrary to the British method that Canada inherited as is the American.

The revolution that Jean-Luc Pépin spoke of had its roots in 1789 just as the French themselves were encouraged by the events of 1776.[3]

Both French and Americans subscribe to the supremacy of law that secures the individual's independence. The British respect the law as protector of their inherent freedom; all are equally responsible for preserving their free institutions.

John Farthing compares the circumstances of the two North American neighbours' development of their western territories. South of the border the Wild West supplied a stage where men could escape from the rigidities of the law and give vent to their natural aspirations: he who shot first became the stuff of legend.

North of the parallel, the Mounties were *there* first, to ensure that development proceeded in an orderly manner. "Nor is there anything more distinctly Canadian. No one has ever regarded Mounties as either English or French, Scottish, Japanese or Australian. They are typically Canadian and they are also the product of the British tradition in this country, of its Canadian expression of peace, order and good government."[4]

That tradition has been at risk in Canada since Lester Pearson established the myth of two founding races. He and contemporaries of his in the Canadian civil service had been exposed to the British in England and formed an attitude that appears to have been part genuine pride in Canada but also part animus toward the British.

Former PEI premier Angus MacLean said once: "As for Pearson, he had a real obsession that you had to sanitize yourself as a country from anything that was British or traditional. A lot of people think that Trudeau started that, but it was Pearson."[5]

In my book *Keeping Canada Together* I described some of the changes that flowed from Pearson's obsession. Outward symbols of Canada's constitutional monarchy were replaced by symbols that conveyed a French tradition.

The Royal Mail became Canada Post, and only after a bitter struggle was Royal kept for the Mounties' title. Trans-Canada Airlines became Air Canada. Government departments were no longer ministries of this or that but Revenue Canada, Employment and Immigration Canada, and so on.

Famous regiments were disbanded to make way for new francophone units. All federal, and increasingly many provincial, government departments were required to provide bilingual receptionists, so that callers were greeted in both languages, often in French first, as was the case with Canadian consulates in the United States and in embassies or high commissions abroad.

Dominion Day, which celebrated Canada's unique history, became the insipid Canada Day which is ignored in Quebec; the "national" day there takes place a week earlier, la fête nationale on the day of St. Jean-Baptiste.

Do the French have a France Day? Of course not. Bastille Day signifies the Revolution that changed France into a republic. Independence Day does the same for the Americans. *Globe* columnist Michael Valpy called Dominion Day "A title synonymous with our very sovereignty."[6]

As recently as January 1997, during a visit to Paris by Prime Minister Chrétien, France and Canada were described as "the two leading francophone countries."[7]

The tragedy of this attempt to straddle two horses is that while it has demonstrably failed to placate the separatists, it has also confused the Canadian majority.

Canadians whose forebears were secure in the British tradition have grown up not only bemused by the vapours of bilingualism and multiculturalism, but, what is far worse, deprived of history and the tradition that evolved with it.

Those Toronto law students were not an isolated case. A dozen years before Dan Gardner wrote, Ontario's governors had decreed that special permission was needed to teach British History as an optional course in high schools after all core requirements had been met.

The provincial education ministry had denied this permission and only two schools in Ontario were still allowed to teach British History as a credit course.

Credits were allowed in Hungarian, Lithuanian, Punjabi, Chinese (Cantonese and Mandarin), modern Greek, German, Italian and Portuguese. All of the courses included the different countries' culture and history; no special permission was needed to teach or register for them; only for British History. In its place, schools were required to offer the option of *Canada's Multicultural Heritage*.[8]

Contrast this *provincial* devotion to multiculturalism in Ontario with the *federal* government's conscripting of bilingualism to the French Canadian cause. When Dr. Ritchie was working in the justice department in Ottawa she decided to brush up her French by taking one of the government's language courses for non-French speakers. She soon realized that although the subject was French, what the instructor was teaching was the French version of Canadian history.

This reconfirmed a point made by Montreal historian Sam Allison 20 years ago when he wrote that "History is combed to reinforce prejudices and to justify discrimination against English Canadians. An unbalanced view of the past is used to justify an unfair present."[9]

Why do people want to come to Canada? It is appropriate that the answer be given by a representative of the people whose own tradition is much older than, and is inextricably mingled with, the British.

Dr. Stephen Stern wrote in *Canadian Jewish News* that they come because of "political and economic virtues [that] are primarily and ultimately Anglo-Saxon in origin...it is the British parliamentary system that is the foundation of many of our freedoms, and the British judicial system with its principles of trial by jury and the presumption of innocence that protect those very freedoms that most of Canada's immigrants find so attractive."[10]

No man can serve two masters. The claim in the Official Languages Act of 1988 that the federal government is charged with "enhancing the vitality of the English and French minority communities in Canada and supporting and assisting their development" is disproved by the evidence of Quebec itself.

There, according to then president of Alliance Quebec, Michael Hamelin, when he appeared before the Commons Committee on Official Languages on May 16, 1996, the anglophones employed in the provincial government are less than one percent of the total.

In the past 20 years more than two-thirds of the English-speaking community's schools have been closed; English-language hospitals have been closed. Mr. Hamelin said: "The experience of the English-speaking community is one of a community that has been slowly losing its institutional base, its population base."[11]

Yet this steady suppression of English in Quebec, which has been winked at by successive Quebec-dominated governments in Ottawa, is compounded by the Chrétien government's implementation of the 1988 Official Languages Act's Sections 41 and 42.

Section 41 charges the federal government with "enhancing the vitality of the English and French linguistic minority communities in Canada and supporting and assisting their development." Section 42 requires the Secretary of State and other ministries "to encourage and promote...the implementation by federal institutions of the commitments set out in Section 41."

The trick pulled in this is that English needs no artificial stimulus; the measures taken against it by Quebec governments are to protect French which is vulnerable not only in Quebec but everywhere else.

Former UN Secretary-General Boutros Boutros-Ghali told a summit of La Francophonie in Benin that French, which once was a language of international diplomacy, had become "a language of translation."

Although about 50 French-speaking nations belonged to the UN, only 10 percent of the books in the UN's main library were printed in French. The UN also had only 4 French databases, compared with 900 in English. On the World Wide Web only 1.8 percent of all homepages are in French. English is the official language of all the world's airports and air carriers.[12]

At the headquarters of Airbus, the consortium of English, French, German and Spanish aerospace companies in Toulouse, the working language is English. In Asia, English has replaced French as the language of business in Vietnam, Laos and Cambodia; in South Africa, Afrikaans is giving way to English, as is French in former French colonies of Central Africa.[13]

In the context of Quebec's competitiveness, its draconic language laws are counter-productive. On a trade visit to Canada, representatives of the Federation of German Industries were "perplexed and miffed" when their questions to a Quebec government official in Montreal who had briefed them in English were answered in French. The board member of one German company called it "a lost opportunity. English is the international business language."[14]

All the doubletalk about government "enhancing the vitality" and "supporting and assisting the development" of linguistic minority communities in Canada means trying to spread the use of French. Prime Minister Jean Chrétien told the 1994 Acadian Conference: "We are going to continue to struggle together because to be French in all the provinces...must continue to be the obligation of our government and we will work with all the effort we have."[15]

In the Commons, October 17, 1995, Mr. Chrétien declared that he had spent his thirty-year career in the House of Commons defending francophones outside Quebec.

Like the red thread through the twine that once distinguished Bridport rope, so does preserving and enhancing the French language infuse every action of Canada's federal government. But whereas the red thread was neutral, a trade mark that spoke for proven strength, the forced infusion of a second language to all of Canada's institutions has only weakened them.

The damaging effect of "equalizing" two different languages in the armed forces was illustrated in chapter 6. That the effect is repeated throughout the institutions of government is a continual drain upon the country's socio-economic strength.

It is not the *existence* of two languages that damages the country; as many languages are spoken daily in Canada as prevail in the countries from which immigrants are drawn. The damage is caused by a misuse of government's monopoly power to force people to use a language they do not need in their lives and careers.

This is a denial of the individual freedom and responsibility which is inherent in the British tradition of the Canadian majority. But it is consistent with the legislated rights and entitlements that are inherent in the French tradition of the regional minority anchored in Quebec.

People come to Canada in the knowledge that the majority language is English and that they will need to learn it to pursue their lives and careers. Of the 224,000 immigrants in 1996, 52 percent spoke English, 4 percent French, and 3 percent spoke both languages. The remaining 41 percent spoke neither English nor French. Of the latter, people who chose to live in Quebec (12 percent of the total) knew that the majority language there is French and that they would need to learn it.

But that, once here, they whose native tongue is English, or who choose to learn the language of the English majority, should be denied advancement in public service, including the armed forces, because of that native ability, or that choice, is a complete denial of the British tradition that attracted them to Canada.

Just as English is the audio-visual expression of the British tradition of inherent freedom and responsibility, so does French express the French tradition of legislated rights and entitlements.

As successive Quebec-dominated Canadian governments used their monopoly power to spread the use of French, so did they spread the statist doctrine that is intrinsic to the French tradition.

Affirmative action, "equalization," redistribution of wealth and incomes, state attempts to manage the economy by countless and ever-mounting interventions - all the built-in handicaps of the intrusive state are a legacy of the French tradition.

A century before the French Revolution, it was a frustrated Paris merchant who responded to the query of finance minister Jean-Baptiste Colbert as to how he could help him and his fellows: he said "Laissez-nous faire."

Policies originated by the Parti Québécois under its founder René Lévesque condemned the province to its dismal economic performance: an unemployment rate that has averaged 1.9 percentage points above the Canadian average and in 1996 was 2.7 points above it; and per capita income some 10 percent below the national average for 35 years.

Quebec economics professor Jean-Luc Migué was quoted as saying that the province's economic ills began with the statist ideology that accompanied the Quiet Revolution in the 1960s: "Ever since we made up our minds that the government was going to direct the Quebec economy, we have had the most statist government in Canada."[16]

The same statist conviction accompanied the "Three Wise Men" to Ottawa and was soon manifested in the redistributive politics of the 1960s and 1970s - and the ensuing debt from which Canada still suffers.

Those policies are embedded in the country's supreme law, imposed by Pierre Trudeau's coup de force. Although the prime purpose, as Trudeau's entourage admitted afterwards, was to entrench the language provisions of the 1969 Official Languages Act, the equality and distributive provisions flowed naturally from the socialist commitment of the Charter's author.

When we take stock of Canada's circumstances we are drawn to a number of conclusions.

Lester Pearson's establishment of the myth of two founding races, together with his importation of "Three Wise Men" from Quebec to advise him, and the findings of the subsequent B and B commission, set the stage for the Great Illusion; namely, that one quarter of the population that lived in Quebec and adhered to the French tradition of law and politics, was equal in all respects to the three quarters that lived in English Canada and adhered to the British tradition.

Pearson's, and subsequently Trudeau's, centralizing policies in Ottawa, which were incompatible with a federal state, inevitably antagonized the Province that was particularly jealous of its exclusive powers under the British North America Act. Thus did centralizing policies - linguistic as well as socio-economic - add fuel to the fire of Quebec's nationalists that Pearson had hoped the "Three Wise Men" would quell.

Subjection to thirty years of Quebec-dominated federal governments and their accompanying imposition of linguistic, cultural and economic policies at variance with the British tradition has confused and demoralized the English Canadian majority to the extent that it appears to acquiesce in this persistent downgrading of its own traditions.

While all this was happening, Quebec's separatists grew steadily stronger until they were able - and the Quebec-dominated federal government allowed them - to form a *federal* separatist party, the Bloc Québécois, which won enough of Quebec's seats in the 1993 election to form Her Majesty's Loyal Opposition in the federal parliament.

(In the federal election of 1997 the Bloc lost some of its seats and was replaced by Reform as the official Opposition.)

Throughout the period, Canada's armed forces suffered the demoralization that necessarily flowed from the policies of Quebec-dominated governments in Ottawa. These were:

- unification, which robbed the three services of their sources of doctrine and strategic thought in separate headquarters;
- denial of funds for re-equipment;
- substitution of political for military/technical criteria in the selection of equipment;
- substitution of language and culture for merit in eligibility for promotion;

- disbandment of famous regiments and their replacement by new francophone units;
- fragmentation, through equality and entitlement provisions of the Charter, of the familial/parental responsibility vis-à-vis officers and NCOs toward those under command that is fundamental to morale;
- above all, a steady erosion of all-round, tri-service combat capability in favour of "peacekeeping."

Overriding the whole sad tale is a fruitless attempt to dampen the fires of nationalism in Quebec by spreading Quebec's way of doing things over the whole country.

Rather than appeasing Quebec's rulers, the resulting federal intrusion into Quebec's legitimate control of its affairs within the province not only antagonized them, it confirmed them in their attachment to separation.

At the same time, a corresponding intrusion into all provincial affairs through the imposition of "universal" social programs led Canada down the primrose path of borrowing and debt which requires drastic measures to recover from.

Central to the "Quebec problem" that bedevils the Canadian polity is the matter of territory which Quebec-dominated governments in Ottawa refuse to consider.

Quebec's separatist governments, as well as their federal counterparts in the Bloc Québécois, persist in the illusion that a separate state of Quebec would be contained within the same boundaries that Quebec enjoys as a province of Canada.

Nevertheless, polls show that substantial majorities of Quebecers, as distinct from their political representatives, agree that the Cree Indians and Inuit who inhabit the vast northern part of Quebec (Rupert's Land) should have the right to stay in Canada if Quebec separated.

The same polls show a majority agreeing that Canadians who live in western Quebec, on Montreal's West Island, and in the Eastern Townships south of Montreal should have the right to "stay with Canada" after secession.[17]

Although the precise allocation of boundaries is a matter of negotiation and eventual settlement, the broad lines have already been determined by the laws of Canada past and by both parties' commitment to the rule of law.

Within still generous boundaries, the nation of Quebec is capable of joining the world's growing list of newly independent states - and joining, after the settling-in period of adjustment, in their prosperity.

In chapter 5, I suggested that once the crucial matter of boundaries had been negotiated, and a settlement had been reached, the two countries would breathe a collective sigh of relief and pursue their affairs in accordance with their respective traditions.

No longer would the Canadian majority be forced to struggle against the built-in headwinds of bilingualism and multiculturalism. English would be the language of choice, as it is elsewhere by virtue of its proven adaptability to changing conditions; but it would not be an "official" language. Canadians would be as free to use languages as they were to pursue lives and careers, all under the protection of laws they learned to respect and within free institutions they felt a responsibility to uphold.

And the former minority that blossomed into a new state of Quebec? Freed from the burden of an intrusive Canadian government, but freed also from the Quebec-inspired doles from that government which sapped their economic strength, the new citizens would finally breathe the air of freedom that their poets and singers have tantalized them with for so long.

And what of the armed forces? We are looking perhaps at ten years during which Canadians and Quebecers might bring themselves to realize that trying to serve two masters is foolish and mutually harmful.

During that time Canada would continue in its commitments to NATO and NORAD. The armed forces would continue their valiant attempt to live with the contradictory requirements of all-round combat capability and "peacekeeping."

If tax and fiscal policies were reformed, the armed forces could be afforded the equipment that would enable them to play a fuller part in the defence of North America.

But their prime duty, during the inevitable disruptions that accompanied the birth of the new state of Quebec, would be to give aid if necessary to the civil power.

This, the role and condition of Canada's armed forces, the topic which is so carefully avoided by Canada's Quebec-dominated governments, is the crux of the matter.

Attaining a peaceful separation of the two nations would call for statesmanship of a high order. It would also call for restraint. Actions that leaned toward an extreme would have to be quashed at once. At all costs, the civil strife to which Canadians are instinctively opposed must be avoided.

On the face of it, circumstances would favour a peaceful settlement; the advantages to both parties are sufficiently persuasive. Nevertheless, extremists on both sides would try to make heroes or heroines of themselves by parading their pet beefs and inflaming whatever mobs they could rally in support.

That is when the police might have to call for back-up from the armed forces, and governments of the day would be obliged to comply.

If the action took place in any of the provinces and territories of English Canada, the forces' task would be straightforward.

The police would know that most of the people supported them and that the action was limited to whatever the extremists were trying to do. The armed services would display whatever force was necessary to support the police and maintain, or re-establish, the peace.

But if the action took place in Quebec, there would be a number of built-in headwinds. The police would not know that a majority supported them. Years of mistrust between various police forces and the people they were supposed to protect would militate against peaceful solutions. Add to this the heady emotions of incipient nationhood, and civil strife becomes more than a possibility.

To envisage that possibility is to face the significance of the role, disposition, and composition of the armed forces.

Their role is to give aid to the civil power, which is represented by the police. The police, many of whose components are heartily disliked by the Quebec populace, might be roused into reprisals. Government might be obliged to call in the armed forces and, here, in the moment of crisis, would the unintended result of foolish policies past come to the aid of the people.

The Royal 22nd Regiment whose predecessors formed a large part of the Canadian Airborne Regiment that was sent to Somalia to restore peace in that forsaken country, would set about keeping the peace in the country that was manifestly their own.

They, the Van Doos, would become the nucleus of the new state's military; their first task to apply the restraining tactics they learned in the "peacekeeping" activities so perfectly suited to Quebec's preference for a more peaceful option in defence matters.

The two countries, of Canada and Quebec, neighbours by force of geography, would have become neighbours by choice.

Chapter 11

The tempting alternative

That scenario, I submit, is one of two possible projections from the state of Canada at the turn of the century, one that contains advantages to both sides. The other, which until recently I had hoped might be attained, is the tempting alternative of a restored federalism.

On Canada's side, however, the latter depends upon the majority's determination to recover both its inherent freedom and political control of its destiny.

The odds against such a development are weighted by the sagging morale I have tried to describe in the book.

It results from Canadians' habitual addiction to government which made them susceptible to the Trudeau coup de force. Imbued with what Herschel Hardin called "a genius for public enterprise" they still looked upon the state as benefactor.

But it made them susceptible also to what Friedrich Hayek described in his classic book about socialism, *The Road to Serfdom*: "The most important change which extensive government control produces is a psychological change, an alteration in the character of the people. This is necessarily a slow affair, a process which extends not over a few years but perhaps over one or two generations."[1]

Continuing with the imposed Quebec model heralds a continuance of the socio-economic condition it has led Canadians into: minority rule by a centralized authority, and a litigious society in which opinion is shaped by state-subsidized factions.

Yet even now, when the imposed Quebec model has landed us with a swollen government apparatus that consumes more than half of the Gross Domestic Product, even now it is tempting to think that the original federalism, which worked so well for a century, could be made to work again.

Felix Morley's praise of federalism's reserving control over local affairs to the localities themselves, together with his conviction that federalism was even more suitable if it "embraced a large area, with strong climatic or cultural differences among the various states therein" - on the face of it, those words seemed doubly appropriate to Canada.[2]

They carry the same sense that guided Canada's Fathers of Confederation in their desire to accommodate the French Canadian minority, and which worked reasonably well until a minority within that minority first invaded, then dominated, the *federal* government in Ottawa - which is where we are today.

But it also presupposes common ground in the way all citizens are to be treated. In Canada the cultural differences between the common law tradition of nine provinces and the civil code tradition of Quebec are not merely strong, they are diametrically opposed.

In a sentence that foreshadowed Mr. Trudeau's Charter of Rights and Freedoms, Felix Morley also wrote of centralized government's "claim that it can provide freedom, and the all too reasonable expectation that what officials provide they will soon begin to define selectively."[3]

The barrier to understanding the cultural differences is much greater than distance. There is very little - less than one percent - cross-translation of novels and non-fiction books, a particularly glaring lack in the pesent context since it denies English Canadian readers access to respected writers in Quebec who "frame the argument for Quebec's independence." Publisher Jack Stoddart was quoted as saying "The French mind is quite different from the English mind."[4]

Canadians who have not lived and worked in Quebec and whose knowledge of conditions there is at best superficial, may accept that Quebec is different, while assuming that the differences can still be accommodated in the federation.

Even the fact that 300,000 anglos have fled the province for English Canada, however disturbing it might be at first glance, is still evidence that they were free to do so in this free country.

It is when we remember the other things that have happened in Quebec that we begin to suspect there is more to the exodus than a random desire to move.

A large part of our failure to appreciate the reasons behind the movement - one of the great migrations of Canadian history - is not only the natural tendency to focus on our own concerns, but also our lack of balanced information.

Complaints of French Canadians in Quebec and scattered else-where are headline material. Rarely mentioned, except from time to time as *criticism* of Quebec's non-French minority, is the denial of fundamental rights to the 20 percent of Quebecers who are not French Canadians.

Nor will that kind of information reach us from relatives or friends who visit Montreal or Quebec City. They are no more aware of the reality of non-French lives in Quebec than we are ourselves of foreigners' lives when we travel abroad.

For that kind of information we have to break through the Pollyanna veil of the left-liberal media and listen to embattled anglos who actually live and work there.

Brian Rogers, architect, friend and long-time correspondent, has spent his whole professional life since 1967 working alongside French Canadian colleagues on the island of Montreal.

Fully bilingual, and, until a dozen years ago, as absorbed in the work as most of us are in our middle years, he began to look behind the scenes. What moved Quebec's political leaders to pass and enforce the language laws? What moved them to restrict the civil rights of the province's 20 percent non-French minority? How could they, as constituent parts of a federal state with a Constitution, in the words of the BNA Act, "similar in principle to that of the United Kingdom," subject an identifiable group of English-speaking citizens to such injustices as those enumerated by Mr. Hamelin?

Let us look at the list of things that have been done by the Government of Quebec in flagrant discrimination against the identifiable group of anglophones in the province.

Many of their schools and hospitals have been closed. They are excluded from employment by the provincial government that forces them to pay taxes to it. They are subjected to draconic laws that treat the English language as a form of visual pollution. Their universities are starved of public funds. Access to English-language schools is restricted along ethnic/hereditary lines that prevent immigrants from attending them.

This is entirely of a piece with the Quebec mode of top down, centralized government that has been foisted on us through the Charter. What is a crime for an individual acting alone, is accepted policy for the government he is forced to obey.

The Quebec government's attack upon this identifiable group reminds us of the Hate Propaganda sections of the Criminal Code we saw in chapter 2. There, I wrote that the sections wouldn't be needed if everyone adhered to Canadians' inherent characteristics, foremost of which is being polite to other people but blunt when necessary.

(I should have written English Canadians' inherent characteristics. As Brian reminds me, "French Canada has cultural and philosophical roots which are different from the rest of the nation...It has no historical roots in the psychology of parliamentary democracy, and no conception of inherent or common law rights.")

How can the Canadian government justify making it a criminal offence for individuals to incite or promote hatred against any identifiable group by *saying* things, when at the same time it allows a provincial government to go a whole lot further by forcing an identifiable group to lose, in Hamelin's words, "its institutional base, its population base" ?

I suggest that if people in the English Canadian majority were asked the question, they would not try to justify it; but would see through the deception and rectify it, if they had the means to do so.

But it doesn't offend the federal government in Ottawa that is supposed to represent that majority. On the contrary, as we saw in chapter 1, the federal government was at pains to pass its Bill C-72 which copied, for the whole country, the arbitrary provisions of Quebec's language law, Bill 101.

This brings us to another of the differences enjoyed by public servants in Quebec - and now through provisions of Bill C-72 by public servants in Ottawa - namely *le droit administratif* that protects government officials from the personal consequences of acts performed in the course of their duties.

In short, it is against the law of the land for one person to *say* bad things about an identifiable group of other persons, but for Quebec's government to *do* bad things to an identifiable group of persons is OK.

That's too much of a difference for me, and it's compounded by the fact that the foisting of the Charter on us (which entrenched the Quebec model) was illegitimate. The government had no mandate from the people to make that organic change and more than two-thirds of the groups and individuals who appeared before the parliamentary committee hearings disapproved of the resolution: 155 out of 227. A Gallup poll released shortly after the Charter proposals were announced showed a majority opposed to them.

In one of his letters, Brian told me he has become convinced that French Canada does not belong in the federation. It is not merely distinct, but far *different* from the other provinces, much more so than any of them are different from one another.

A federation must have certain common standards of fundamental rights; Quebec's are 180 degrees apart from Canada's and so are those expressed in the fraudulent Charter. In short, a federation which cannot, or whose Quebec-dominated federal government refuses to, enforce common standards of civility is fatally flawed and does not deserve to survive; it is nothing more than a league of convenience, a trading bloc, not a country or nation.

That view, readers will notice, has been expressed by Quebec Premier Lucien Bouchard, but it also takes us back to the intentions of Messrs Pearson and Trudeau to shift Canada into "a new kind of internationalism" during this "transitional period in world history." Pearson's appeasement of Quebec, Trudeau's "consuming aversion" to Quebec nationalism, English Canadian political leaders' obsession with an unattainable "national unity," the intransigence of Quebec's own political leaders - all these have worked to exemplify the law of unintended results.

In their separate ways, all of those leaders (some well-meaning, some the reverse) have achieved nothing but to confirm the truth written a century ago by Jules-Paul Tardivel in his novel *Pour la Patrie*: "There are too many basic differences between the two races who inhabit this country to be able to make them into a truly united nation."

We might be looking at ten years during which Canadians and Quebecers come to realize that trying to serve two masters is as foolish and mutually harmful in the civil field as it is in the military. Surely it is not too much to hope that Canadians will also realize that Quebec's statist model is not only out of date but that it doesn't work, and that imposing it upon the whole of Canada was a grave mistake; scrapping it and downsizing our grossly inflated government apparatus is a task we shirk at our peril.

That is why the majority needs to stiffen its collective spine and demand a similar resolve of its political leaders.

Clearly it will look in vain to Jean Chrétien or any other MP from Quebec. The Quebec model that Trudeau imposed on Canada is their model too and they see nothing wrong with it.

Nor can any of them at the federal level even consider the idea of Quebec's secession. The moment it gained popular acceptance so would their legitimacy as Members of Parliament vanish: they would be out of a job. Hence the Chrétien government's desperate appeal to the Supreme Court.

Now it is perfectly understandable that Jean Chrétien will go to great lengths to keep Quebec in Canada. But the Canada he wants to keep it in is the one he set out to change ("We will change Canada...change Canadian institutions", he boasted in the Commons, October 6, 1980) - in short, the Canada we have now.

Not only is it in his personal interest to oppose secession, it is also in line with the French mode of centralized authority that he and Trudeau imposed on us and that his quasi-dictatorial power as Prime

Minister enables him to enjoy.

This is not the place to speculate on the kind of negotiations that would follow Quebec's departure, nor on the kind of constitutional arrangement Canadians might decide upon afterwards.

The challenge to Canada's majority is to understand what has been done to it.

NOTES

Chapter 1

1. Somerville, *Trudeau*, p. 194. After "an intensive study of everything [Trudeau] had written over the years" Erik Nielsen concluded that "he had the philosophical convictions of a Marxist-Leninist at the most, and at the very least was an extreme left-wing socialist." *The House Is Not A Home*, Macmillan of Canada, 1989, p. 181.

2. Somerville, *Trudeau*, p. 204.

3. Armstrong, *Farewell*, pp.23-4, in which the author describes the widespread misunderstanding of the phrase's origin. See also Thorson, *Wanted*, p. 153: "The historical fact is that the French Canadians did not request any such equality of partnership during the Confederation discussions and no such equality was conferred on them."

4. The usage of "civil rights" was in the sense of parties suing over a private interest, as distinct from public (e.g. criminal) law, where the state prosecutes to serve a public interest. See Hunter, *Three*, p. 43.

5. *Globe*, March 17, 1987.

6. (British) House of Commons Debates, March 3, 1982, columns 364 and 377.

7. Clarkson & McCall, *Trudeau*, pp. 280-1.

8. US Gross Debt in 1996 was $5,207,298 million (Dept. of Treasury Fact Sheet OPC-27.1, November 6, 1996). US population as of 07-01-96 was 265,283,783 (US Census Bureau). This equals $19,629 per capita. A conservative estimate of Canada's unfunded pension liability is about $900 billion to give a total debt in 1996 of $1.7 trillion (*Globe*, 04-02-97). This equals $56,666 per capita. Actuaries estimate there is a $1.2 trillion deficit in Canada's health and social programs, half of it due to health care. (Ontario Teachers' Pension Plan CEO Claude Lamoureux in the *Sunday Sun*, March 8, 1998.)

9. Rummel, *Death*, p. 70.

10. Sédillot, *Le coût*, quoted in *Chronicles*, June 1989, "The Cost of Revolution - England & 1789" by George Watson.

11. Trudeau, *Federalism*, p.126.

12. Campbell, *Governments*, p. 93.

13. Letter from Joel Aldred to the author.

14. (British) House of Commons Debates, March 3, 1982, column 364.

15. Dicey, *Law*, pp. 226-7 and 254.

16. Johnson, *Modern*, pp. 274-5.

Chapter 2

1. Hore, Edward. "Caught in the Act." *Saturday Night*, September 1989, p. 25.

2. Herrnstein, Richard J. and Murray, Charles. *The Bell Curve: Intelligence and Class Structure in American Life.* New York: The Free Press, 1994, pp.642-3.

3. Rummel, *Death*, pp. 8-9. The 42 million figure against Stalin is for the years 1929-53. From 1917 to 1987, Rummel estimates that the Soviet state killed 54,769,000 of its citizens.

4. Veith, *Modern Fascism*, p. 26.

5. Historian Curtis Cate in *Chronicles*, July 1997.

6. Johnson, *Modern*, pp. 293-4. Also, while he admitted that both systems were collectivist, socialistic and opposed to liberalism, Mussolini drew on Fascism's being "rooted in the great cultural tradition of the Italian people; Fascism recognizes the right of the individual, it recognizes religion and family. National Socialism, on the other hand, is savage barbarism...Murder and killing, loot and pillage and blackmail are all it can produce." Toland, *Hitler*, p. 355.

7. Johnson, *Intellectuals*, p. 319.

8. Kulaszka, Barbara. *The Hate Crimes Law in Canada 1970-1994: Effects and Operation*. A private paper circulated in November 1994.

9. *Globe*, April 7, 1995. Also, in an address to a combined luncheon of the Empire and Canadian Clubs, April 21, 1997, Judge Abella said that "Only courts have the independence from electoral judgment to risk controversy in enforcing rights." *Toronto Star*, April 24, 1997.

10. Abella, Rosalie. "Equality at Work and Home," *Policy Options*, December 1985, p. 32.

11. Chief Justice Dickson in *R. v. Oakes* [1986] 1 S.C.R. 103, at 136, quoted in David P. Shugarman, "Ideology and the Charter," *federalism and political community: Essays in Honour of Donald Smiley*, p. 315. In his classic book, *Democracy and Leadership* (first published in 1924), Irving Babbitt wrote that "Social justice...means in practice class justice, class justice means class war and class war, if we are to go by all the experience of the past and present, means hell."

12. *federalism*, p. 232. For further reading on the Charter's revolutionary effects, see Leitch, *Freedom*.

13. *Globe*, June 8, 1993.

14. Kelly, Karen. "Visible Minorities: a diverse group," in *Canadian Social Trends*, Summer 1995, Statistics Canada Catalogue 11-008E, pp. 2-8.

15. Trudeau, *Federalism*, p.161. Also *Cité libre*, April 1962.

Chapter 3

1. Mathews, Don. "Does Big Mean Bad? The Economic Power of Corporations." *The Freeman*, February 1996.

2. *Ford Motor Company of Canada v. The International Union, United Automobile, Aircraft and Agriculture Implement*

Workers of America (U.A.W. - C.I.O), 1944-48 Para 18001 (Rand Formula), contained in CCH Canadian Limited Canada Wartime Labour Relations Board Decisions.

3. Before the 1997 federal election, Public Service Alliance of Canada President Daryl Bean said that federal civil servants who took unpaid leave to campaign for candidates would have their pay made up by the union. Such candidates would have to sign a pledge "to support free collective bargaining and pay equity, to protect public service by government employees - instead of contracting out - and to support social programs such as pensions and full health care...Each candidate will have to sign the pledge." It was no secret, he said, "that most of the candidates will be New Democrats." *Toronto Star*, April 14, 1997.

4. Howard Levitt in the *Toronto Star*, December 6, 1993.

5. Peter Cook, *Report on Business*, August 30, 1993.

6. *Globe*, October 5, 1995.

7. *Toronto Star*, October 28, 1995.

8. *Globe*, April 13, 1996.

9. *Globe*, April 17, 1996.

10. Christina Blizzard, *The Sunday Sun*, March 31, 1996.

11. *Toronto Sun*, October 24, 1996.

12. NCC, *Consensus*, Vol. 10, No. 4, Vol. 11, Nos. 2 & 4, Vol. 12, No. 5, Vol. 14, No. 1.

13. *Lavigne v. O.P.S.E.U. [1991] 2 S.C.R. 211 at 304.* In 1997, when Judge La Forest retired, Prime Minister Jean Chrétien replaced him with Mr. Justice Michel Bastarache, who said in an interview that when he was teaching law or writing about it: "I had trouble keeping my interest for long in a subject unless I thought it had some kind of social relevance to what was really happening. Here, I feel there is so much that can be done that will have this kind of effect." *Maclean's*, October 13, 1997.

14. The gap between learned judges' sympathy for unions and public opinion was evidenced in a study by social trends analyst Dr. Reginald W. Bibby. 90 percent of respondents disagreed that union membership should be a condition of employment; 60 percent disagreed that where a union was in place new employees should be required to join it; more than 80 percent of all respondents, including union members, said that use of union dues for non-union purposes should be voluntary; 86 percent, including 78 percent of current union members, believed that confrontation is not necessary - unions and employers are capable of cooperating. "Canadians and Unions: A National Survey of Current Attitudes." Toronto: Work Research Foundation, March 1997.

15. *Financial Post*, May 31, 1994.

16. *Globe*, November 1, 1997; *Sunday Sun*, February 8 and February 15, 1998.

17. *Globe*, June 27, 1998.

18. *Toronto Star*, February 17, 1998.

Chapter 4

1. *Globe*, October 16, 1996.

2. *Globe* economics editor Bruce Little quoting Statistics Canada 13-210-XPB, May 19, 1997; Margaret Philp in the *Globe*, February 13, 1998; Robert Matas in the *Globe*, June 10, 1998.

3. From 1977 to 1996, Canada's unit labour costs grew at almost twice the rate of the US (109% vs. 57%), while productivity growth was barely more than half (36% in Canada vs. 70% in the US). *Globe*, June 27, 1998.

4. Farano Green. *Tax and Fiscal Commentary*, Vol. 10, No. 6, January 1997.

5. *Globe*, February 8, 1996.

6. Sandra Cordon in the *Toronto Star*, March 6, 1998.

7. *Toronto Star*, January 2, 1996; *The Taxpayer*, Vol. 9, No. 2, 1997.

8. *Toronto Star*, April 23, 1996, letter from David G. Long, of Campbellcroft, Ontario.

9. *Report on Business*, June 24, 1996, letter from Les Morrison, of Burlington, Ontario.

10. *Globe*, June 26, 1995.

11. *Globe*, February 8, 1996.

12. Bruce Little in *The Globe and Mail*, November 27, 1995.

13. Ferguson, John R. *Pathway to Prosperity: A single tax solution to Canada's productivity and debt problems.* Draft 5, January 1996, of a 177-page private paper, it informs much of the thrust of this chapter and is gratefully acknowledged.

14. In my book *Keeping Canada Together* I suggested that the levying of income taxes should be reserved to the provinces; Ottawa would be dependent upon them for revenue. After years of research, Robert Marquis has shown that the idea is implicit in the BNA Act, and is writing a book on the subject.

Chapter 5

1. *Toronto Star*, November 4, 1995; *Sunday Sun*, May 11, 1997.

2. *Toronto Star*, November 11, 1995.

3. Lecker, Robert, "The writing's on the wall", *Saturday Night*, July/August, 1996.

4. *Legion* Magazine, May/June 1997, p. 64. In his column headed "Remembrance Day is just an anglo thing," Montreal writer Benoit Aubin noted that "Three English-language networks seem to go overboard with Remembrance Day, while their French counterparts all but ignore the event." *Globe*, November 15, 1997.

5. Gibbon, *Decline*, p.44.

6. Gardner, T. Dan. "A Vanishing War." *Globe*, May 3, 1995.

7. Santayana, *Life*, Vol. 1, p. 284.

8. Rose, J. Holland. *The Personality of Napoleon*. New York, 1912, p. 200. Quoted in Durant, Will and Ariel. *The Age of Napoleon*. New York: Simon and Schuster, 1975, p. 247.

9. Montgomery, Bernard L. *Memoirs*. London: Collins, 1958, p. 105.

10. Cessford, Mike. "Land Force Command Faces Prime Imperatives." *Vanguard* Magazine, Vol. 1, No. 4, December 1995.

11. *Toronto Star*, May 8, 1996.

12. *Globe*, May 16, 1997.

13. Shaw and Albert, *Partition*, pp. 55-135. Also p. 25: "Since the part of Quebec south of the St. Lawrence River was never acknowledged as part of New France before the Conquest, and since most of that part of the province is English by early grants, and by treaties with Indian chiefs, and by the Treaty of Utrecht of 1713 signed by France, as well as by priority of settlement, the Canadian negotiators would be in a much stronger position diplomatically and juridically than the separatist negotiators."

14. Shaw and Albert, (pamphlet) *Partition - The Geo-Political Consequences of Quebec Sovereignty*, 1992, The Preparatory Committee for the Partition of Quebec, PO Box 431, Cote St. Luc, PQ, H4V 2Z1.

15. In the House of Commons, May 21, 1980, Prime Minister Trudeau said: "This is why, on May 14, I solemnly undertook to launch the constitutional renewal and never stop working at it until Canada finally has a new constitution." His two "prerequisites for change" were "a federal Parliament with real powers applying to the country as a whole" and "that a charter of fundamental rights and freedoms be entrenched...and that it extend to the collective aspects of these rights, such as language rights." Commons Debates, May 21, 1980, pp. 1263-4.

16. Reid, *Lament*, p. 113. In a separate study, *The Cost of Official Bilingualism to Canada*, December 1996, Toronto chartered accountant J. S. Allan calculated the average cost, taken over the 27 years since 1969, at $30 billion per year.

17. *The Toronto Star*, May 6, 1997, quoting Quebec political scientist Pierre Drouilly.

Chapter 6

1. Armstrong, *Farewell*, pp. 82-83. Also, "[The Imperative Staffing Principle] was deceptively simple to implement; the manager of any group in government, no matter how small, had to be bilingual once a single position in that group was designated as bilingual." p. 153.

2. Porter, *Retreat*, pp.21-28.

3. *Globe*, April 17, 1992, and *Toronto Star*, May 25, 1998.

4. APEC Newsletters, May, 1992, January 1994, March 1994, May 1994, January 1996.

5. Peter Worthington, "The Bosnian diaries," in *The Sunday Sun*, January 12, 1997.

6. APEC Newsletter, January 1996.

7. *Globe*, October 13, 1995.

8. Porter, *Retreat*, p. 93.

9. *Toronto Star*, November 1, 1995.

10. *Sunday Sun*, April 7, 1996, letter from Michael J. Smith of Mississauga.

Chapter 7

1. Stethem, Nick. "No Battlefield Can be 'Politically Correct'." *Vanguard* Magazine, Vol. 1, No. 3, Summer 1995. See also David Code, "'Obsessive Secrecy' For The Military A New Posture," in *Vanguard*, December 1996.

2. Gwyn, *Northern*, p. 38.

3. Trudeau, *Memoirs*, p. 37.

4. Porter, *Retreat*, p. 2.

5. Gilbert, W.S. *The Gondoliers*, Act I.

6. Paul Koring in *The Globe and Mail*, February 10, 1998.

7. Total government expenditures rose from 29.6 percent of GDP in 1966 to 51.6 percent in 1992. *Globe*, December 30, 1997.

8. James F. Dunnigan and Austin Bay. *A Quick & Dirty Guide to War, Briefings on Present and Potential War*. New York: William Morrow, 1985, pp. 392-6.

9. *Ibid*, p. 379.

10. Speer, *Spandau*, pp. 339-340.

11. Richards, *Hardest*, pp. 301-2. See also L.S.B. Shapiro, "The Bombers Blazed A Short Cut To Victory" in *Maclean's* Magazine, June 1, 1945.

12. Despite the much lower number of total casualties, the high proportion of aircrew can be compared to the losses of Britain's and Canada's elite in the Great War. 55,573 RAF aircrew, including 17,101 Canadians serving with the RAF or RCAF, were killed in World War II. (The Canadian Army suffered 17,683 battle casualties.) 38,834 officers of the British Empire forces lost their lives in World War I. John Terraine wrote: "[B]y and large RAF aircrew were exactly the same type of men as the officers of 1914-18." See English, *Cream*, p.144.

13. The Bomber Harris Trust, *Battle*, p. xv.

14. Motion court Judge Robert Montgomery cited *Knupffer v. London Express, [1944] A.C. 116* and especially Lord Atkin at p. 121 that "in order to be actionable the defamatory words must be understood to be published of and concerning the plaintiff" - in short that to say "all lawyers are thieves" is not actionable because no lawyer is singled out. But Lord Atkin's immediately following words said that "it is irrelevant...that two or more persons are called by some generic or class name. There can be no law that a defamatory statement made of a firm, or trustees, or tenants of a particular building is not actionable, if the words would reasonably be understood as published of each member of the firm or each trustee or each tenant." The filmmakers defamed all of the aircrew in Bomber Command generically and as a class of "50,000 Canadians serving in the campaign to bomb Germany" and each one was, and is still, identifiable in the records.

15. *Court of Appeal for Ontario, Grange, LaBrosse and Abella JJ.A. C17615, June 13, 1995.*

Chapter 8

1. Vallières, *Assassination*, p. 172.

2. Gwyn, *Northern*, p. 135.

3. *Ibid.*, p. 110.

4. Trudeau, *Memoirs*, p. 22.

5. *Maclean's* Magazine, October 28, 1996.

6. *Toronto Star*, September 23, 1996.

7. Anthony Keller in *The Globe*, October 25, 1996.

8. *Lavigne v. O.P.S.E.U. [1991] 2 S.C.R. La Forest at 19.*

9. *Toronto Star*, October, 25, 1996.

10. *Toronto Star*, November 8, 1996.

11. *Toronto Star*, October 26, 1996.

12. *Globe*, August 24, 1996. A year later, "Public sector employees constitute 25 percent of the work force, 50 percent of pension plan members and close to 70 percent of pension assets and contributions." (Terence Corcoran in *Report on Business*, November 14, 1997.)

13. *Report on Business*, July 11, 1996.

14. Thatcher, *Downing*, p. 378.

15. *Globe*, October 26, 1996.

16. *Toronto Star*, October 26, 1996.

17. Sowell, Thomas. *Marxism: Philosophy and Economics*. New York: Quill, William Morrow, 1985, pp. 212-3.

Chapter 9

1. Pupetz, Ron (Ed.). *In the line of duty: Canadian Joint Task Force Somalia, 1992-1993*. Ottawa: Department of National Defence, 1994, pp. 23-37.

2. Milberry, Larry. "Air Transport Group Hard at Work in Somalia." *Wings* Magazine, Issue 3, 1993.

3. *Line*, p. 7.

4. Nelson, Derek. *The Intelligencer*, April 14, 1993. (Thomson News Service Foreign Affairs Correspondent Derek Nelson wrote a number of columns from Somalia.)

5. *Line*, p. 7.

6. *Ibid*, p. 8.

7. Nelson. *Nanaimo Daily Free Press*, April 10, 1993.

8. *Line*, pp. 266-7.

9. *Globe*, October 16, 1996.

10. *Globe*, December 18, 1996.

11. Nelson. *Guelph Mercury*, April 23, 1993.

Chapter 10

1. Peyrefitte, *Trouble*, p. 248.

2. *Ibid.*, p. 209.

3. "The essential difference between the American Revolution and the French Revolution is that the American Revolution, in its origins, was a religious event, whereas the French Revolution was an anti-religious event." Johnson, *History*, p. 117.

4. Farthing, *Freedom*, p. 132.

5. *Globe*, September 30, 1982.

6. *Globe*, July 1, 1989.

7. *Toronto Star*, January 22, 1997.

8. NCC, *Consensus*, Vol. 7, No. 4, July 1982

9. Allison, *French*, p. 55.

10. Stern, Stephen. "Immigrants Should Honour Canada's Heritage." Reprinted in *The Frankford Advertiser*, October 5, 1995.

11. APEC Newsletter, Vol. XIX, No. 8, October 1996.

12. *Globe*, December 4, 1995, and May 22, 1997; *Sunday Sun*, May 25, 1997.

13. *Globe*, May 14, 1997 and July 13, 1997. The 1997 Francophonie summit was held in Hanoi, Vietnam, the former French colony where "less than 1 percent of the population speaks French. The second language of choice is English." *Globe*, November 14, 1997.

14. *Globe*, May 27, 1997.

15. Halifax, *The Chronicle-Herald*, October 16, 1994. Three years later, when Ottawa allotted additional funds to Canadian publishers, the money was split equally between French and English publishers. *Toronto Star*, November 22, 1997.

16. Greg Ip, in the *Globe*, October 26, 1996. Also, since 1968, all major labour relations decisions in the Quebec construction industry have been made by the provincial cabinet and imposed by orders-in-council (decrees). In March 1997, a carpenter was paid $22 an hour basic wage plus $12 an hour fringe benefits, compared to $18 plus $6 in Toronto, and US$10 - US$15 an hour in Syracuse, NY. - "Destructive impacts of the closed shop on the Quebec construction industry" by Roger J. Bedard for the Work Research Foundation, March 1997.

17. William Johnson in *The Financial Post*, May 23, 1997.

Chapter 11

1. Hayek, *Road*, pp. xi-xii.

2. Morley, *Freedom*, p. 5.

3. Ibid., p. 305.

4. Ray Conlogue in the *Globe*, October 15, 1998.

BIBLIOGRAPHY

Allison, Sam. *French Power.* Richmond Hill: BMG Publishing Ltd., 1978.

Armstrong, Joe C.W. *Farewell the Peaceful Kingdom.* Toronto: Stoddart, 1995.

The Bomber Harris Trust. *A Battle for Truth.* Agincourt, Ontario: Ramsay, 1994.

Campbell, Colin. *Governments under stress.* Toronto: University of Toronto Press, 1983.

Clarkson, Stephen, & McCall, Christina. *Trudeau and Our Times.* Toronto: McClelland & Stewart, 1990.

Dicey, A. V. *The Law of the Constitution.* Indianapolis: Liberty Fund, 1982.

English, Allan D. *The Cream of the Crop: Canadian Aircrew 1939-1945.* Montreal: McGill/Queen's University Press, 1996.

Farthing, John. *Freedom Wears A Crown.* Vancouver: Veritas Publishing, 1985.

Gibbon, Edward. *The Decline and Fall of the Roman Empire - The Portable Gibbon.* New York: Viking, 1952 (Dero A. Saunders, Ed.).

Gwyn, Richard. *The Northern Magus.* Toronto: McClelland & Stewart, 1980.

Hayek, Friedrich A. *The Road to Serfdom.* 2nd ed. Chicago: University of Chicago Press, 1976.

Hunter, Ian. *Three Faces of the Law.* Mississauga, Ontario: Work Research Foundation, 1996.

Johnson, Paul. *A History of the American People.* New York: HarperCollins, 1997.

Johnson, Paul. *Intellectuals*. New York: HarperPerennial, 1990.

Johnson, Paul. *Modern Times: The World from the Twenties to the Eighties*. New York: Harper & Row, 1984.

Morley, Felix. *Freedom and Federalism*. Chicago: Henry Regnery Company, 1959.

Peyrefitte, Alain. *The Trouble with France*. New York: Alfred A. Knopf, 1981.

Porter, Gerald. *In Retreat*. Ottawa: Deneau and Greenberg, 1979.

Reid, Scott. *Lament for a Notion*. Vancouver: Arsenal Pulp Press, 1993.

Richards, Denis. *The Hardest Victory*. London: Hodder & Stoughton, 1994.

Rummel, R.J. *Death by Government*. New Brunswick, NJ: Transaction, 1994.

Santayana, George. *The Life of Reason*. New York: Simon and Schuster, 1981.

Sédillot, René. *Le coût de la révolution française*. Paris: Perrin, 1987.

Shaw, William F., and Albert, Lionel. *Partition*. Montreal: Thornhill Publishing, 1980.

Shaw, William F., and Albert, Lionel. *Partition - The Geo-Political Consequences of Quebec Sovereignty*, 1992. The Preparatory Committee for the Partition of Quebec, PO Box 431, Cote St. Luc, PQ, H4V 2Z1.

federalism and political community: Essays in Honour of Donald T. Smiley. Peterborough: broadview press, 1989.

Speer, Albert. *Spandau: The Secret Diaries*. New York: Macmillan, 1976.

Thatcher, Margaret. *The Downing Street Years.* New York: HarperCollins, 1993.

Thorson, J.T. *Wanted: A Single Canada.* Toronto: McClelland & Stewart, 1973.

Toland, John. *Hitler.* Ware: Wordsworth Editions, 1997.

Trudeau, Pierre Elliott. *Federalism and the French Canadians.* Toronto: Macmillan of Canada, 1968.

Trudeau, Pierre Elliott. *Memoirs.* Toronto: McClelland & Stewart, 1993.

Vallières, Pierre. *The Assassination of Pierre Laporte.* Toronto: James Lorimer, 1977.

Veith, Gene Edward, Jr. *Modern Fascism: Liquidating the Judeo-Christian Worldview.* St. Louis: Concordia, 1993.

INDEX

Luftwaffe, 111
Luxembourg, 75, 81

M

Macdonald, John A., 3
MacLean, Angus, 147
Magna Carta, 114, 141
Mao Tse-tung, 13, 21-22, 142
Marchand, Jean, 2
Marquis, Robert, 168
Martin, Paul, 64
Marx, Karl, 129
Masse, Marcel, 88
Mathieu, Carol, 93
McClelland, Jack, 25
McKid, John, 16
McPherson, A., 111
Media, 5, 14, 15, 22-23, 26, 32,
    67, 95-96, 100, 104, 129, 159
Medicare, 14, 50, 56
Michigan, 45, 129
Migué, Jean-Luc, 152
Milberry, Larry, 173n
Mobile Command, 88
Mogadishu, 132-138
Moi, Daniel Arap, 137
Monarchy, 11, 148
Monopoly, 40, 41, 43, 45-48,
    126, 151-152
Montgomery, Bernard, 169
Montreal, 5, 35, 36, 77, 84, 88,
    110, 118, 149-150, 154, 158-
    159, 168, 176-177
Morale, 2, 22, 37, 77-79, 87, 91-
    92, 94, 99, 102-103, 112,
    115-116, 120-121, 139-140,
    154, 157
Morley, Felix, 1, 157-158, 177
Morrison, Les, 168n
Mulroney, Brian, 24, 27, 36, 56,
    128
Multiculturalism, 23-25, 31, 34,
    36-37, 148-149, 155
Munich, fwd

Murphy, John, 123
Murray, Charles, 19, 164
Mussolini, Benito, 22, 164

N

Nairobi, 132, 133
Napoleon, 79, 169
Nasser, Gamal Abdel, 22
National Citizens' Coalition, 49
National Film Board, 113
National Union of Provincial
    Government Employees, 50
Nationalist Party, 23
NATO, 75, 81, 103, 107-108,
    110, 115, 117, 155
Nazism, 78, 120
Nelson, Derek, 173n
New Brunswick, 76, 85, 177
New Class, 5-6
New Democratic Party, 28, 45,
    48
New York, 129
New Zealand, 126
Newfoundland, 94
Nobel Peace Prize, 75
Non-governmental organizations
    (NGOs), 133
NORAD, 81, 107, 117, 155
Normandy, 100, 112, 137
Nova Scotia, 89
Nuremberg, 78

O

October Crisis, 117, 120
Offensive Action, 79
Official Languages Act, 6-7, 10,
    17, 149, 150, 152
Ogaden, 133
Oka, 119
Ontario, 1, 19, 23, 25, 36, 42, 45-
    47, 49-50, 52-53, 58, 60, 63,
    72, 85, 113-114, 121-122,

103, 105, 107-109, 118-120,
128, 145-146, 148, 152-153,
157-158, 161, 163-165, 169,
171-172, 176, 178

U

Underground economy, 60, 70,
72
Unemployment, 36, 45, 60, 66,
77, 126, 152
Unification, 143, 153
United Nations, 67
United States, 12, 43, 57, 75, 81-
82, 85, 96, 104-105, 111,
117, 147-148
United States Army Air Force,
111
United States Marine Corps.,
108
USAF, Military Transport
Service (MATS), 110

V

Vallières, Pierre, 119
Valour and the Horror, 113
Valpy, Michael, 148
Vancouver, 35-6, 137
V-E Day, 1
Veith, Gene, 178n

W

Wales, 84
War Measures Act, 118
Wealth, 10, 14, 27, 30, 38, 40,
55, 58, 63, 65, 69-70, 127,
152
Welfare state, 12, 33, 37, 58, 60,
77, 143
Western Guard, 23
Westminster, Statute of, 6
White, John, 49
Wilson, Bertha, 49-50

Windsor, 42
Winnipeg, 81
Work Research Foundation, 167,
175-176n
World War I, 171
World War II, 16, 78-9, 95, 98,
110, 114, 171
Worthington, Peter, 90, 170

Y

Yugoslavia, 74, 76, 100, 105